REVEALING ANTIQUITY

•18•

G. W. Bowersock, General Editor

NEW HEROES IN ANTIQUITY

From Achilles to Antinoos

✦

CHRISTOPHER JONES

Harvard University Press
Cambridge, Massachusetts
London, England
2010

Library of Congress Cataloging-in-Publication Data

Jones, Christopher P., 1940–
New heroes in antiquity : from Achilles to Antinoos / Christopher Jones.
    p.   cm. —(Revealing antiquity ; 18)
Includes bibliographical references and index.
ISBN 978-0-674-03586-7
1. Mythology, Greek.   2. Gods, Greek.   3. Superheroes—Greece.
    4. Heroes—Greece.   5. Greece—Religion.   I. Title.
BL785.J66 2010

292.2'11—dc22   2009011505

Contents

Acknowledgments

This book began as a series of four lectures that I had the honor of delivering at the Collège de France in March 2001. I am very grateful to those who made my stay there so memorable, especially Professors Marc Fumaroli and Gilbert Dagron, and to those who attended my lectures and improved them by their comments, particularly Jean-Louis Ferrary. Since then I have spoken on the topics of this book in several places, the University of Chicago, the University of Toronto, Yale University, and Dumbarton Oaks Research Center, Washington, D.C., and to these audiences too I am grateful. Most of the research has been done in the incomparable surroundings of the Institute for Advanced Study, Princeton, and I am indebted to the many people who made my stays there possible and fruitful. My greatest thanks, however, are due to the person who has read with a searching but always kindly eye almost everything I have written, my dear friend Glen Bowersock.

List of Illustrations

NEW HEROES IN ANTIQUITY

Introduction

✦

In 422 B.C.E., the Spartan general Brasidas was mortally wounded while fighting an Athenian force outside the city of Amphipolis in Thrace, and his troops carried him into the city, where he died soon afterwards. The historian Thucydides, who sometimes allows the religious activity of humans into his narrative, but never divine agency, shows unusual interest in the details of Brasidas' funeral and subsequent commemoration. The citizens fenced off his monument, and thereafter worshiped him "as a hero," honoring him with a special sort of bloody sacrifice and with annual games around his tomb. Ascribing the foundation of the city to him, they obliterated all traces of the actual founder, the Athenian Hagnon, thus removing one founder from their official memory and substituting another.

This book is a study of such "new heroes." Behind the process described by Thucydides at Amphipolis lie centuries of social and religious evolution that go as far back as the Bronze Age before going forward into Late Antiquity. I will begin by tracing the two main streams that feed into the creation of such "new heroes" as Brasidas: first, the commemoration of heroes in high poetry and, second, the worship of the petty divinities or "heroes" of particular localities. These two streams meet in the conversion into heroes of those who have fallen in war, or given their lives in the service of their communities in other ways. Thereafter I will follow the extension of the notion of hero to others recently dead, women as well as men: philosophers, poets, family members, civic benefactors. Above all, I hope to modify a commonly held view that the word "hero" when applied to such new heroes in later centuries was a meaningless compliment, like "dearly beloved" or "of blessed memory," or even a mere circumlocution for "the late." This will also involve asking how belief in the traditional heroes such as Hector and Achilles coexisted with belief in these new, fully human, heroes, especially in the period of the Roman Empire. Finally, I will inquire how the traditional heroes fared in the Christian world of Late Antiquity, and whether ancient hero-cult influenced the Christian cult of the saints.

Poetic Heroes

✦

The first classic of Greek literature, Homer's *Iliad,* begins with a bitter contrast between the life of heroic combat and its joyless reward after death.

> Sing, goddess, of the wrath of Achilles, son of Peleus,
> which brought numberless sorrows upon the Achaeans;
> many brave souls of heroes it hurled to Hades,
> and themselves it made prey for all kinds of dog and bird.[1]

Homer's use of the word "hero," and his application of it above all to warriors who fight and often die, was decisive for later generations. He and his near contemporary Hesiod helped to shape all later thought about the divine order; these two, said Herodotus, "first taught the Greeks the descent of the gods *(theogoniê),* and gave to all their several names."[2]

Despite Homer's frequent use of the word "hero," later Greeks wondered what exactly he meant by it, especially in the *Iliad:* did he use it only for the leaders of Homeric society, the kings, or did he use it of all who fought at Troy, Greeks as well as Trojans? (The answer is surely the second.) Plato connected the word with *erôs* or the verb *eirein,* "ask," and others such as St. Augustine derived it from the goddess Hera, a view that has found support in modern scholarship.[3]

A partial clue to the word's meaning, or at least its use, before the Greek rediscovery of writing in the eighth century comes from Mycenaean tablets written in Linear B, two of which refer to offerings made to a *tiriseroe,* a word probably meaning "thrice hero." This "thrice hero" therefore received worship long before the composition of the Homeric epics, in which heroes play an enormous role, but are not worshiped. The tablets reveal little else, and the "thrice" may suggest a being triply strong or valiant, a heroized ancestor three generations back, or something else not yet understood.[4]

The English word "lord" is in many ways the best rendering of *hêrôs*, and this too has undergone transformations that conceal its etymological origin. It derives ultimately from two words of Old English meaning "bread" (*hláf*, "loaf") and "guardian" (*waerd*, "ward"). Thanks to a continuous tradition of literacy, the word can be followed from the coalescence of these two elements to its modern form, where the decisive influence on its meaning is the accidental fact of its selection to translate the Latin *dominus*. In the same way, etymology is less helpful than usage for understanding what "hero" meant in early poetry and what it came to mean for later generations.[5]

The *Iliad* uses "hero" principally for the combatants at Troy, more often Achaeans than Trojans, and Hesiod applies it similarly to the Seven against Thebes and to the Greek combatants at Troy. Though the word never lost an association with war and other forms of combat, the *Odyssey* also applies it to men such as the peaceable king Alcinoos, to one of his elderly nobles, to a king of Sidon in Phoenicia, and to the bard Demodocos. Thus, whatever the etymology, the usage in the Homeric poems is closer to "lord" than "warrior." "Lord" was appropriate for ancient warriors and to others who lived in a glorious past, when men were often the offspring of mixed marriages between gods and humans, such as Achilles and Aeneas. In that past, gods mingled with humans as they did on the plain of Troy or on Odysseus' Ithaca, and men performed superhuman feats such as ridding the earth of monsters, returning alive from the underworld, or founding peoples, cities, and families.[6]

As well as using "hero" more broadly than the *Iliad*, the *Odyssey* gives a different presentation of the nature of heroes. When Odysseus goes down to the underworld in Book XI, he can call the shades to converse with him by shedding the blood of sheep into a trench and allowing the dead to drink. Moreover, in keeping with the large role played by women in the *Odyssey*, he observes the souls not only of warriors such as Agamemnon and Achilles but also of celebrated women such as

Alcmena, the mother of Heracles, and Epicaste, the mother and wife of Oedipus. These women, though not called "heroines," are nonetheless the "wives and daughters of heroes." Some heroes do not go to Hades at all. Menelaus, the husband of Helen and thus the son-by-marriage of Zeus and Hera (since Helen was the daughter of Zeus and Leda), is promised a different fate by the sea-divinity, Proteus.

> But for you it is not destined, Menelaus whom Zeus fosters,
> That in horse-rearing Argos you should die and meet your lot,
> But to the Elysian plain and the ends of the earth
> The immortals will escort you, where fair Rhadamanthus is,
> And where existence is easiest for humans:
> No snow is there, nor heavy storm, nor ever rain,
> But always the high-whistling breezes of Zephyr
> Come sent from Ocean to refresh human beings,
> Since you have Helen and for them you are Zeus' son by marriage.[7]

Though the Homeric poems do not refer explicitly to the cult of heroes, they contain adumbrations of the cult that was offered to them later, though whether they encouraged or shaped such cult is disputed.[8] The funeral games that Achilles celebrates for Patroclos resemble the recurrent "tomb contests" *(epitaphioi agônes)* that take place later around the tombs of heroes. So also Odysseus sacrificing to the shades in the underworld digs a pit and pours a libation to all the dead, first with milk mixed with honey *(melikrêton)*, then with wine, and lastly with water; thereafter he sacrifices a black ram and a black ewe, cutting their throats over the pit. Several of these items, the use of honey mixed with milk, the slaughter of victims and the pouring of the blood into the ground, resemble the rite for the dead called in later literature *enagismos,* "tabooing."[9]

The idea of a blessed afterlife received powerful and vivid expression from Hesiod, who in the *Works and Days* gives a famous account of the five races of mankind. The immortals created the first, golden race, in the time of the primal god Cronos. The men of this race live on after death as "fine spirits upon the earth *(daimones esthloi epichthonioi)*, the guardians of mortal human beings." The immortals also created the second, silver race, "much worse," whose members fought among themselves and dishonored the gods, so that Zeus, the son of Cronos, dismissed them. "But since the earth covered up this race too, they are called blessed mortals under the earth *(hypochthonioi makares thnêtoi)*—in second place, but all the same honor attends upon these as well." Next Zeus made a third, bronze race, whose members also fought among themselves and "went down nameless into the dank house of chilly Hades."

The fourth race, "more just and superior" to the last one, Hesiod himself may have inserted in an older scheme. This, which was also Zeus' creation, is "the godly race of men-heroes, who are called demigods." These are the warriors who fought before Thebes "for Oedipus' sheep" and the Achaeans who fought at Troy. "There the end of death shrouded some of them, but upon others Zeus the father, Cronos' son, bestowed life and habitation far from human beings and settled them at the limits of the earth; and these dwell with a spirit free of care on the Islands of the Blessed beside deep-eddying Ocean—happy heroes, for whom the grain-giving field bears honey-sweet fruits flourishing three times a year." Hesiod seems to imply that the heroes' blessed existence after death is not due only to their status as demigods but is also a reward for their goodness in life. For the fifth race, his own, he speaks in the tones of a prophet and almost always in the future tense, foretelling nothing but misery and injustice. Yet it must be those of this race whom he imagines as guarded by the "spirits" of the golden race and as honoring the blessed dead of the silver one, while he does not say how the heroes of the previous age were related to his own.[10]

A poem generally believed in antiquity to be a work of Hesiod, but probably of the sixth century, is the *Catalogue of Women,* composed to form a sequel to the real Hesiod's *Theogony.* Byzantine sources refer to it as *Catalogue of Heroic Women (Gynaikôn hêrôikon katalogos)* or *Heroic Genealogy (Hêroikê genealogia),* since it lists the "tribe of women" who had intercourse with gods, and thus created several lines of heroic genealogy stretching down to the time of the Trojan War. It was known only in prose summaries and some short quotations until papyri discovered in the course of the twentieth century revealed long stretches, so that the total is now over a thousand lines. In none of the surviving fragments is any of these women called a "heroine," though at least two achieve immortality: Phylonoe, the daughter of Tyndareus and Leda, and Iphimede (better known as Iphigeneia) whom Artemis made "immortal and ageless" by pouring ambrosia on her head and so turning her into "Artemis by the Road" *(Einodia),* more usually known as Hecate. The poem continued to be read well into the Roman period, from which most of the papyri come, and must have influenced later thinking about female heroes, "heroines." A woman from Mesembria in Thrace called Julia daughter of Nicias claims on her tombstone that she is now "the god Hecate; once I was mortal, but am now immortal and ageless," an evident borrowing from the *Catalogue of Women.*[11]

In what survives of the poem, the chief "heroine" is Helen. The fifth book related at length how many heroes who were later to fight in the Trojan War contended for her hand and swore to help the winner if anyone stole her from her husband; Achilles, though, did not take part either in the wooing or the oath, being still a youth under the tutelage of the centaur Chiron. After the birth of Helen's first "unexpected" daughter, Hermione, Zeus "was eager to annihilate most of the race of speech-endowed human beings, a pretext to destroy the lives of the demigods." The text is here fragmentary, and the links of thought obscure, but it seems that the father of the gods intended some of the heroes to live as before in bliss and "far from humans," while devising "painful war" between immortals and mortals. There follows a vivid description of a storm, perhaps the storm that delayed the Greek ships at Aulis, and then in a long and very mutilated passage the unknown poet told of a snake that gives birth "in a hiding-place in the earth to three offspring in the third year." The connection is not clear, but the snake is constantly associated with heroes in later art and literature, and its presence here might suggest that a new generation of heroes was to enter the world later than the Trojan War. It is in fact in the sixth century, the supposed date of composition, that such new heroes begin to be attested in historical time.

Just as papyri have restored long stretches of the Hesiodic *Catalogue of Women,* so more recently they have yielded parts of a hitherto unknown work, or passage from a longer work, of the early fifth-century lyric poet Simonides. The subject is the final land-battle of the Persian War, Plataea, and some have seen the poem as implying the worship of those who took part in the battle as heroes. The order of the fragments is not assured, but the first may be an invocation to Achilles, "son of the sea-nymph, glorious in your fame"; on this followed an account of his death from an arrow shot by Alexander (another name of Paris), which the gods avenged by allowing the Greeks to destroy Troy. These gained "immortal glory" from Homer, who caused "the short-lived race of demigods" to be known to later generations, and Simonides now invokes the Muse as he seeks to immortalize the Greeks who defeated Persia. The protagonists of the episode, so far as it survives, are the Spartans under their leader Pausanias, who marched "leaving the Eurotas and Sparta . . . with the horse-taming son of Zeus, the Tyndarid heroes and mighty Menelaus, the leaders of their ancestral city." The passage leaves much unclear. Certainly the poet invokes Achilles in a way that implies that he can still hear and lend his aid; and the Tyndarids Castor and Pollux together with Menelaus accompany the Spartans as they march out, though whether they do so in visible form, perhaps as images, or merely by lending a favorable but unseen presence, the poet does not say. Above all, it is unclear whether he regards Pausanias and perhaps other of the combatants as new heroes, or potentially able to become such after their deaths. Though it was not unexampled by 479 for those who had fallen in war to be treated as heroes, the poem cannot be taken as evidence of such heroization; certainly not for the regent Pausanias, who was still alive and was to be put to death in Sparta some ten years later.[12]

The Theban poet Pindar stands at the boundary between the archaic age and the classical. He is the first to formulate the triple distinction between gods, heroes, and men in the famous opening to his *Second Olympian:* "Hymns that rule the lyre, what god, what hero, what man shall we proclaim?" For Pindar the paramount hero is Heracles, the "hero god," the only person to whom he applies this expression; this reflects the special status of Heracles as the semidivine benefactor of humanity who died in agony and yet lives with the Olympians as "the son-by-marriage of Hera." Later in the century, Herodotus argues that there are really two persons called Heracles, one of whom is immortal and thus called "Olympian," the other who receives *enagismos* as a being below earth.[13]

Whereas the cult of heroes is merely adumbrated in Homer and is absent from Hesiod's description of the heroic race, in Pindar it is prominent, largely because his victory poems concern the four major contests *(agônes),* Olympia, Pythia, Isthmia, and Nemea, which were closely connected with the heroes. At Olympia, and not only during the four-yearly games, Pelops "partakes of splendid blood offerings *(haimak-ouriai)* as he reclines by the course of the Alpheos, having his much-attended tomb beside the altar thronged by visiting strangers": this probably implies the sacrifice of the victim with the throat cut so as to bleed into the earth, as Odysseus sacrifices in the underworld. At Delphi, Neoptolemos, the son of Achilles, has his own enclosed area *(temenos)* and there, "beside the god's well-walled temple, he dwells as a rightful overseer of processions honoring heroes with many sacrifices." In the poet's own Thebes there is a similar nocturnal sacrifice with many victims in honor of Heracles: "for him we citizens . . . prepare a feast and a newly built circle of altars, and multiply burnt offerings for the eight bronze-clad men who died, the sons that Megara, Kreon's daughter, bore to him. For them at sunset the flame rises and burns all night long, kicking heaven with its savor of smoke." Protesilaus, the first Greek to die at Troy, has a *temenos* at his native Phylaka in Thessaly, on which an ancient commentator observes that the citizens honored him with a "tomb-contest" *(epitaphios agôn).* In the Catalogue of Ships the "lesser" Ajax brings his troops from Opous in central Greece, and for Pindar an Olympic victor from the same city places his crown on Ajax's altar. The same Catalogue tells how Tlepolemos, a son of Heracles, fled his native Argos after killing his uncle, and settled in Rhodes, from where he led the Rhodians to Troy: for Pindar he is compensated for his "piti-ful misfortune" when "as if a god" he receives "a procession of rich sac-rificial flocks and the judging of athletic contests." This presumably means, not that he is a god, but a hero who presides at contests held in his honor like Neoptolemos at Delphi.[14]

Pindar also makes explicit an important development in the nature of heroization, already adumbrated by Hesiod, whereby excellence or virtue *(aretê)* becomes a passport to heroic status. The power to confer immortality still belongs to the gods, as the Seasons *(Hôrai)* and Earth *(Gaia)* made the son of Apollo and the nymph Cyrene immortal, and Athena made Diomedes "an immortal god." Yet immortality is not just an arbitrary gift, but is inseparable from fame *(kleos)* and moral or martial excellence *(aretê).* In a difficult passage, the poet says that those who have lived three times free from all acts of injustice on earth and below earth "take the path of Zeus to the tower of Cronos," where they live in a kind of paradise, a land of cool breezes and flowering plants. These blessed ones include Peleus and Cadmos, both of them married to goddesses, but also Achilles, whom his mother brought here "after persuading the heart of Zeus with her prayers": this is a marked contrast with the *Odyssey,* in which Achilles complains bitterly to Odysseus about the hateful gloom of the underworld.[15]

In a quotation preserved by Plato, Pindar links moral virtue and heroism not only for heroes of myth but for others, kings, wise men, and athletes. "But for those from whom Persephone accepts requital of the ancient grief [he perhaps refers to her grief at the murder of her son Dionysos], in the ninth year she returns their souls to the upper sunlight; from them arise proud kings and men who are swift in strength and greatest in wisdom, and for the rest of time people call them sacred heroes." This seems a clear reference to the doctrine of the transmigration of souls, best known through Plato's Myth of Er in the tenth book of the *Republic.* It is uncertain what Pindar's source is for this view, whether Pythagoreanism, Orphism, or mystery religions such as that of Eleusis, and without the context we cannot tell whether he named any of the "kings and men" who had now become "sacred heroes."[16]

Though Pindar mentions many women of heroic times who united with gods or heroes to produce heroic or divine offspring, he does not talk of them as "heroines." But at the beginning of the eleventh *Pythian,* he imagines Apollo at Thebes summoning "the native host of heroines *(hêrôidas)* to assemble in common gathering," the first appearance of this word in Greek. These are presumably the many minor figures associated with Theban myth, for example Androclea and Alcis, two sisters who gave their lives to achieve victory for Thebes when Heracles was leading it in a war against Orchomenos; these were buried in a local sanctuary of Artemis and still received cult in Pausanias' day.[17]

The only person of historical time whom Pindar calls a "hero" is a Greek king on African soil. Three of his extant poems celebrate victors from Cyrene, the mainly Spartan colony founded on the coast of modern Libya in the later seventh century. Two honor Arcesilas IV, the last king of a dynasty that had descended from the original founder, Aristoteles of Thera, who was usually known by a secondary name of Battos, "Stammerer." The fourth *Pythian,* Pindar's longest poem, tells at length how the god Triton gave to one of the Argonauts, Euphamos, a mysterious clod of earth that symbolized his descendants' rule over Cyrene. As the *Argo* sailed on, the waves washed the clod off the ship and it floated to Thera, from where Battos, a descendant of Euphamos in the seventeenth generation, led the first settlers to Cyrene. The next poem alludes to a different tradition by which, a generation after the Argonauts, the sons of the Trojan Antenor came to Libya after the war and settled a site called the "Hill of the Antenoridai" near the later Cyrene, where they were "welcomed with sacrifices" by Battos and his followers; an ancient commentator correctly understands "welcoming" to mean, not that Battos lived at the time of the Trojan War, but that in the poet's day the citizens of Cyrene offered regular cult to the descendants of Antenor. Pindar continues: "He [Battos] founded larger sanctuaries for the gods, and laid down a paved road, straight and level, to echo with horses' hoofs in processions that honor Apollo and bring succor to mortals. And there, at the end of the agora, he has lain apart since his death. He was blessed while he dwelt among men, and afterward a hero worshiped by his people. Apart from him before the palace are the other sacred kings whose lot is Hades; and somehow with their minds below the earth they hear of the great achievements sprinkled with soft dew beneath the outpouring of revel songs—their own happiness and a glory justly shared with their son Arcesilas."[18]

Pindar thus links Battos' piety in life, in particular his reverence for Apollo, and his later heroization. This, and the emphasis on his separateness in death, recalls Hesiod on the posthumous life of the heroes, just as Pindar's adjective "blessed" *(makar)* recalls Hesiod's use of the same word for the men of the silver race. Battos is "a hero worshiped by his people"; though dead, he lies in the part of the city most frequented by the living, while his successors lie elsewhere, and are now in Hades, where "somehow" they hear of their descendants' prowess. Pindar's words have found confirmation in archaeology. Italian excavators have found a tumulus on the east side of the agora that dates to the early sixth century and appears to be the original tomb of Battos and the one mentioned by Pindar. Later, probably in the next century, the tumulus was partially destroyed, and replaced with a new one that covered a rectangular stone chamber. This, decorated with a statue of the founder, was henceforth regarded as what Catullus called the "sacred sepulcher of ancient Battus."[19]

If the original meaning of "hero" was similar to the English "lord," designating not a fixed class but any person regarded by the speaker as especially venerable, it is natural that in these early centuries of literate Greece it could be applied in different ways. For Homer and Hesiod it refers above all to the warriors of "heroic times," not necessarily the offspring of gods but nonetheless exalted beings in comparison to the present race of mortals. In the *Odyssey* and in Hesiod such beings can earn a special place after death, not the dark, pitiless Hades of the *Iliad*, but a bright region located vaguely in the West or in Elysium. In Pindar, who is perhaps influenced by the philosophy of the late archaic period, virtue in a broad sense, the excellence of athletes as well as kings and "wise" men, can earn them a similar place of light and happiness as their reward. All these ideas help to influence the idea that the recently dead, especially those who display their *aretê* by giving their lives in war, can also become heroes, new heroes for their communities as Battos was for his.

CHAPTER 2

Local Heroes

✦

B esides Brasidas, the only hero named by Thucydides is a certain Androcrates, who enters the narrative when his *hêrôon* forms a point of topographical reference. He is a local hero of Plataea, the city of southern Boeotia near which the Greeks defeated the Persians in the great battle of 479, and Thucydides' predecessor Herodotus had already mentioned his sanctuary *(temenos)* when narrating the battle. It is thanks to this event that a much later Boeotian, Plutarch, supplies almost all that is known of Androcrates, who was one of several "originators" or founding fathers *(archêgetai)* of the city. Yet for all his obscurity, Androcrates rather than Brasidas typifies the heroes of the fifth century, "little local deities who never rose to wide or universal greatness."[1]

The relation between these little deities and the heroes of early poetry is not easy to discern. Singers must have woven songs about them, sometimes bringing them into narratives of great events of the past, such as the expedition of the Argonauts and the Trojan War. But the Panhellenic poems that celebrated the great heroes such as Achilles and Odysseus also had their influence on cult, leading communities to worship heroes made famous in song. A clear instance is Protesilaos, mentioned in passing by Homer for his death on the eve of the Trojan War, whose grave the citizens of Elaious opposite the Troad identified with a prehistoric mound near their shore, even though he also enjoyed cult in his native Thessaly and elsewhere. In the third century of the Christian era, this mound served as the setting for the only work surviving from antiquity that is wholly devoted to the heroes, the *Heroikos* of Philostratus.[2]

Archaeology suggests that some of the Homeric heroes received cult as early as the eighth century. Excavation of a small cave on Ithaca has revealed a continuous history of usage from the eleventh or tenth century to the first before our era. Fragments of tripod-cauldrons of Bronze Age date were found there, as well as many figurines, often of female figures, and a terracotta mask inscribed "vow to Odysseus" from the late Hellenistic period. The first excavators identified the cave with the one sacred to the Naiads where Odysseus hid the gifts given him by the Phaeacians, "tripods and cauldrons . . . gold and tireless bronze and well-made garments." Hence, so they inferred, Odysseus received cult on Ithaca from an early date, perhaps even before the composition of the *Odyssey*. It seems more likely that the cave began as a cult-site of the nymphs and came to include Odysseus through the influence of Homer. The first clear evidence for his cult on Ithaca is of the late third century, and consists of games celebrated by the community, *Odysseia*, and a public meeting-place called the *Odysseion*.[3]

One of the most fertile sources of such cult is Laconia. At Therapne east of Sparta, Agamemnon, Menelaus, and Helen have cult-places that can be traced back archaeologically at least to the seventh century. The site was occupied in Mycenaean times and then abandoned, though traces of occupation could have suggested to later inhabitants that this was the home of a Homeric hero, and perhaps specifically the grave of Menelaos and Helen. The earliest certain evidence for their cult is dated about 675–650, a bronze *aryballos* (oil-flask) dedicated to Helen as wife of Menelaos, and the first shrine was built about a hundred years later. At several other sites around Sparta, there were shrines of Achilles as well; at one of these the locals claimed that the hero once visited Sparta seeking Helen as his wife. Though the *Catalogue of Women* had claimed that Achilles was too young to be one of Helen's suitors before the War, a legend grew up that the pair lived after death in bliss on an island in the Black Sea, a theme exploited by Philostratus in the *Heroikos*.[4]

Perhaps because of its early cult of Homeric heroes, Sparta and its colonies are a fertile source for the heroization of the recently dead. Sparta itself has yielded a remarkable series of so-called hero-reliefs, though none of them actually uses the word *hêrôs*. They typically show a man and a woman seated, sometimes with their names inscribed, and receiving offerings from figures that must represent their surviving family-members. The best known, the "Chrysapha relief" now in Berlin, shows a man and woman enthroned, with a large snake rising up behind them. Facing them stand two small figures, the man holding a cock and an egg, the woman a flower and a pomegranate (Pl. 1). At first taken to be gods, the seated figures were later recognized as heroes, all the more since the snake was often associated with the heroic dead. A fragmentary relief of similar style shows only the feet of the two male and female divinities and part of the snake, but unlike the Chrysapha relief it is inscribed with the name "Chilon." This must be the celebrated Spartan statesman of the mid-sixth century, later numbered among the Seven Sages of Greece, and if so, this relief comes from the *hêrôon* of Chilon observed by the traveler Pausanias many centuries later.[5]

Dorian colonists led by Sparta planted a colony on the island of Thera in the ninth century, and excavations have revealed a cult of Achilles there going back at least to the early sixth. Thera was also the mother-city of Cyrene, where the settler-king Battos was worshiped as a hero from an early date, and it is also one of the most fertile regions of posthumous heroization in the Hellenistic period. Similarly the Spartan colony of Tarentum was noted for allowing its dead to be buried within the walls, not as usual outside them. A monument from Tarentum of the fourth century shows a deceased warrior in total nudity, with a snake at his feet and behind him another animal that is frequent in monuments of heroes, a horse (Pl. 2).[6]

Selinous in northwestern Sicily has recently produced a text of major importance for the cult of such local heroes, dated about the middle of the fifth century. Inscribed on a lead tablet, it contains a series of pre-scriptions for sacrifice. The first preserved part concerns sacrifices for the ancestors in the third degree *(tritopatores)*, some of whom are "im-pure" *(miaroi)*, others "pure" *(katharoi)*. While the "pure" receive sacri-fices "as to gods" (that is, of the same kind as those offered to gods), the others do so "as to heroes." The "impure" receive an offering of wine "through the roof" (of their tombs), and the ninth part of a sacrificial victim burned whole. For this act the text uses the rare verb, *katagizein*, which implies the total destruction of the thing offered as a source of *agos*, which denotes a religious power that may be either negative or

Pl. 1. Relief from Chrysapha, Laconia (courtesy of the Antikensammlung, Saatliche Museen zu Berlin. Photo credit: Bild archiv Preussischer Kulturbesitz/ Art Resource, NY)

Pl. 2. Monument of a young warrior, Tarentum (by permission of the Ministero per i Beni e le Attività Culturali—Soprintendenza per i Beni Archeologici della Puglia)

positive, "sanctity" or "impurity." By contrast, the "pure" receive a fully grown victim and a mixture of honey and wine *(melikraton)*. In a later part of the same inscription, a man who has been freed from ritual pollution may placate the "Avenger" *(Elasteros),* probably a subterranean Zeus of Vengeance, by sacrificing "as for the immortals, but he must slaughter towards the ground"; that is, he must cut the victim's throat so that the blood flows into the ground, just as Odysseus does in the underworld. In this text, therefore, the "heroes" exist below earth, receive offerings of wine in their tombs, and are assimilated to "impure" ancestors. In such a context "impurity" denotes the association with death and the underworld that affects both deceased ancestors and heroes, insofar as the two groups are different. Hence what is consecrated to them becomes *enagês*, "possessing *agos*," and demands different treatment from that which is offered to the gods above.[7]

While the Selinous tablet uses the compound verb *katagizein* to denote this form of consecration, the more usual compound, having virtually the same meaning, is *enagizein*. In early texts this is used intransitively, "to make a taboo offering," and when it comes to have a transitive sense means approximately "to taboo." Herodotus uses it when distinguishing the sacrifice that Greeks made to Heracles "as to a hero" from what they did for him as a god, while for sacrifice to the god Heracles he uses the general, "unmarked," term, *thuein*. While *enagizein* and its related words, *enagismos* ("rite of tabooing"), *enagisma* ("thing tabooed"), are used differently by different sources and changed their meaning in the course of centuries, their persistent link with heroic sacrifice marks the heroes as beings "below the earth" *(chthonioi)*, though the inference sometimes drawn from Herodotus that they were necessarily "chthonic," and that there was a sharp distinction between sacrifice to them and sacrifice to the Olympians, is no longer tenable.[8]

Next to Sparta and its colonies, the city that offers the most evidence for the cult of local heroes is its great rival, Athens. From an early date, the Athenians worshiped their first king Erechtheus who, having sprung from the seed spilled by Hephaestus while assaulting Athena, was "earth-born" and is sometimes represented as a snake. A passage perhaps added at a late date to the Catalogue of Ships in Book II of the *Iliad* speaks of Athens as "the land of great-hearted Erechtheus, whom Athena, daughter of Zeus, once nurtured, but the grain-giving earth bore him; and she settled him in Athens, in her own rich shrine, and there the youths of the Athenians, as the years roll on in their courses, seek to win his favor with sacrifices of bulls and rams." By the fifth century, it had become an acknowledged tradition that Erechtheus was an early king of Athens who led the city in a successful war against Eleusis;

in Euripides' partly preserved play *Erechtheus*, he gives his life on behalf of his citizens, and in return Athena orders that "a precinct be built in mid-city, with stone surrounds," that is, the well-known Erechtheion on the Acropolis, and that "he shall be called August Poseidon surnamed Erechtheus, by the citizens in their sacrifices of oxen."[9]

In the long period of aristocratic supremacy at Athens, culminating in the tyranny of Pisistratus and his sons in the late sixth century, there were families *(genê)* and other groups such as the "brotherhoods" *(phratriai)* that had their own cults, often centered on a minor divinity or hero: one such clan is the Boutadae descended from Boutes, the first priest of Poseidon Erechtheus.[10] After the expulsion of Hippias the son of Peisistratus, the Alcmaeonid clan, which he had banished, came to power, and its leader, Cleisthenes, undertook a series of reforms that laid the basis for the radical democracy of the next century. Among his reforms was the replacement of the previous four tribes *(phylai)* into which the people of Athens had been divided by ten new ones. Each of these was named after an "eponym," a local hero who gave his name to the new tribe, and whose own name was chosen by Apollo of Delphi from a list of one hundred. Erechtheus led the list of ten, while the other nine were lesser-known figures of Attic myth, with the exception of Ajax "the Greater," cousin of Achilles, who was included because of his family's origin from Salamis. These ten heroes received a monument in the Athenian agora, though each of the tribes worshiped its eponymous founder at various sites within the city and outside, Erechtheus, for instance, in his old shrine on the Acropolis.[11]

The population of Attica lived in "demes," small agglomerations that were either quarters of the city and its suburbs or villages and towns outside, for instance, the Potters' Quarter (Kerameis) northwest of the Dipylon gate or Marathon on the east coast. Cleisthenes now rearranged the demes to make a total of a hundred and thirty-nine and assigned each to one of the ten tribes, ensuring that each tribe consisted of demes from different parts of the territory. Some of these demes existed before his reforms, while others were new creations and received new names, but whether new or old, all had distinct patterns of worship, often involving heroes and heroines. Thus Boutes, a son of Erechtheus, was originally the ancestor of the priestly clan of the Boutadae, but became the hero of a new deme of the same name created by Cleisthenes, whereupon the clan changed its name to Eteoboutadai, "Real Boutadae."[12]

An early "cult-calendar" of Athens, an inscribed list of sacrifices to be performed on specific days or in specific months, dates from the first part of the fifth century and lists sacrifices performed by the whole citizenry; among the divinities honored are a "hero" and "heroine." Another calendar, from the second quarter of the fifth century, belongs to some group below that of the city; here the divinities include "the two heroes in the plain," probably a male and female hero worshiped in the central plain of Attica, the southern part of which included Athens.[13]

Later calendars fill out the dry details of these early ones. A late fourth-century inventory of the property of an unnamed hero includes a couch, a mattress and other bedding, a set of silver drinking vessels, and a tray for serving barley-cakes. A text dated to the very end of the same century concerns the leasing of a sanctuary of an otherwise unknown hero, Egretes, by his worshipers, here called *orgeônes*. The lessee, Diognetos, who is perhaps one of the members, may live in the sanctuary and make repairs or improvements to the buildings, and he must look after the trees growing within it and replace any that die. "But when the *orgeônes* sacrifice to the hero in [the month] Boêdromiôn, Diognetos is to leave the house containing the sanctuary [a room housing the cult-statue] open, and (provide) a shelter, a cooking-pot, couches, and a table to fit two couches for three persons." Here again the cult of the hero involves conviviality and merrymaking, a banquet as much as a ritual. This type of cult is illustrated by Attic reliefs that show a male reclining at a banquet and receiving gifts from his votaries; the food is normally of a simple kind, fruits and small cakes, quite different from the bloody sacrifice offered to heroes such as Pelops at Olympia. Though such reliefs have often been understood to show funerary banquets, when they indicate the principal subject they usually call him by the simple "hero," sometimes with an additional qualification such as "healer" *(iatros)*, "founder" *(archêgetês)*, "ancestral" *(patrôos)*.[14]

A now-lost play of Menander, not far away in date from the inscription of Egretes, had the title *Hero*. The title-character, called "hero-god" in the cast-list, does not appear in the surviving fragments, but came on early in the play and perhaps explained the background of the plot. To judge by the role of Pan in the surviving *Dyscolos*, he may have assured the audience that he would watch over the main characters and bring about a happy ending. Even if the Athenians of the late fourth century softened or sentimentalized their local heroes, they continued to believe in them and to pay them worship.[15]

This Athenian respect for the traditional heroes appears also from their reluctance to apply the name of hero to the ordinary dead. In the grave reliefs from Attica and elsewhere that commemorate the dead with clearly heroic motifs, for example, the snake entwined in the branches of a tree or around an altar, the word "hero" does not appear until the Hellenistic period, and *hêrôon* is not used for a family tomb before about 200 B.C.E. A college of *hêrôstai*, "hero-worshipers" who gather to celebrate the memory of the recently dead, appears about the middle of the first century, well after such groups had begun to appear elsewhere.[16]

The creation of new heroes is a practice that combines two strands: the exaltation of heroes in the poetic tradition, especially the poems of Homer and Hesiod, and the related but separate cult of local heroes, most of them "little deities" like Androcrates at Plataea and Egretes at Athens. Not surprisingly, these two strands meet in the heroization of recently fallen warriors, "war-heroes" in the fullest sense, of whom Brasidas is the most conspicuous example, but by no means the first.

CHAPTER 3

Warriors and Patriots

⊹

The first heroes of Greek literature are those who died on the battle-field of Troy, and from archaic times down to Late Antiquity there was a strong link between the idea of warfare, especially death in battle, and the concept of the hero. As Greek "colonies" *(apoikiai)* began to take root far from the homeland from the eighth century on, fighting and death became part of the struggle to establish a firm foothold on foreign soil. It is approximately in the sixth century that the first fusion is visible be-tween the heroism of high poetry and the worship of those who had fallen in battle or died as the "founders" *(oikistai)* of successful colonies.

The first known of these is Battos at Cyrene in the late seventh century, whom, as already discussed, Pindar commemorates as a hero venerated by his citizens. The historian Herodotus, always interested in unusual or ex-ceptional religious practices, records other of these early heroizations. Late in the sixth century, the Athenian Miltiades son of Kypselos, uncle of the more famous victor of Marathon, left Athens out of dislike for the Pisis-tratids, and became the absolute ruler *(tyrannos)* of a fiefdom in the Thra-cian Chersonese (the modern Gallipoli peninsula), whose affairs he guided with success until his death. In Herodotus' day the inhabitants of this unofficial colony still "sacrificed" *(thuousi)* to Miltiades "as is right for a founder *(oikistês),* and [held] an equestrian and athletic contest *(agôn)* for him." Herodotus uses the general term *thuein,* and not a more techni-cal term such as *enagizein,* because in this context he is only interested in the fact of sacrifice, not in the manner of its performance. Sacrifice and contests are two of the surest marks of heroization, and this treatment of an Athenian aristocrat in a half-barbarian settlement contrasts sharply with the reluctance of the Athenian state to heroize its own dead.[1]

Herodotus records a similar act of heroization in a community only partly Greek. About a generation after Miltiades, Dorieus, the younger son of king Anaxandridas of Sparta, resentful that his half-brother Cleomenes had succeeded to the throne, left his homeland to found a colony in the west. After various adventures he and his followers were killed in battle near Segesta, but one of them, Philippos of Croton, "an Olympic victor and the handsomest man of his day, received from the Segestans what no other man did: they set up a heroic shrine *(hêrôon)* at his tomb, and propitiate *(hilaskontai)* him with sacrifices." Here again the sacrifices are presumably blood-offerings, but Herodotus' word "propitiate" points to another aspect of heroic status, the power of a hero to harm as well as to protect. Philippos was all the more likely to attain this status after death because of his personal beauty, a sign of divine favor.[2]

Although heroization of the recently dead is unusual at Athens, there is a notable exception. Athenian memory credited the lovers Harmodius and Aristogiton with the fall of the Peisistratid regime; they had in fact been executed after assassinating Hipparchus, Peisistratus' younger son, in 514, while the end of the regime came only four years later with the expulsion of Hipparchus' brother Hippias. Like other states in transformation, the young democracy put the deaths of its own champions to use. The "tyrannicides" *(tyrannoctonoi),* as they came to be called, began to receive the mistaken credit of "liberators" of Athens, and their descendants received privileges from the state such as exemption from certain public services.[3]

In this transformation of the historical record, the younger of the two, Harmodius, whom Thucydides mentions as strikingly handsome, tended to eclipse Aristogiton, and is always named first. He became the subject of *skolia* or drinking songs, and a number of these survive, one of which compares him to Homeric heroes and imagines him as transported to Isles of the Blessed, as Hesiod imagines the "the godly race of men-heroes":[4]

> Dearest Harmodius, you cannot be dead:
> no, they say you are in the Isles of the Blessed,
> Where swift-footed Achilles is,
> and, they say, Tydeus' son, Diomedes.

In addition to this informal veneration, the Athenians soon set up statues to the tyrannicides, which after the occupation of 480 the Persians carried off as spoils; the city then commissioned new ones, and when the Great King returned the old ones, both pairs stood in the center of the agora, with a space left around them in this area crowded with monuments. But the main focus of their cult was the recently instituted public burying-ground (*dêmosion sêma*) in the Kerameikos (Potters' Quarter), an elongated space stretching from the Dipylon Gate northwest of the Acropolis to the grove of the hero Hecademos, more usually remembered as Plato's "Academy," and their burial place, perhaps a cenotaph, was near the entrance to this grove. Here the polemarch, originally a magistrate for war but later having only civilian duties, offered *enagisma* to the two as heroes.[5]

By contrast with Herodotus, his younger contemporary Thucydides describes only one act of heroization, that of Brasidas in 422, but he does so in remarkable detail for a historian so averse to bringing religion into his narrative.

"After this all the allies in full armor followed Brasidas, and buried him at public expense in the city in a spot facing the present agora. Thereafter the Amphipolitans, having enclosed his memorial, make blood-sacrifice to him as a hero, and have given him honors in the form of contests and yearly sacrifices. They ascribed the colony to him as their founder, after demolishing the buildings of Hagnon and obliterating any reminder of his foundation, considering that Brasidas had been their savior, and under the circumstances also courting the alliance with Sparta for fear of the Athenians, and (considering) that Hagnon, because of their hostility to Athens, would not regard the honors with the same advantage to themselves or the same pleasure (to himself)."[6]

Amphipolis had been an Athenian colony since 437, when Hagnon, son of Nicias, had been sent out to occupy it for the purpose of controlling the rich silver mines of the nearby Mount Pangaios. In 424, during the first phrase of the Peloponnesian War, the Spartans sent Brasidas to detach Athens' Thracian possessions, of which Amphipolis was the most valuable, and he brought it over to the Spartan alliance in the following winter, while Thucydides as general successfully held its harbor city of Eion for Athens. (As a historian, his interest in Brasidas is partly due to his own involvement in these events.) He does not say that the Amphipolitans decided to make Brasidas a hero, but only that they began to sacrifice to him "as a hero," to acknowledge his new status by ritual act. Nor does he speak of Brasidas' heroization as a religious innovation, but as proof of his magnetism and its effect on the power-rivalry between Athens and Sparta. It is true that Aristotle refers in passing to a law "to sacrifice to Brasidas," but this implies only that the citizens bound themselves by law to commemorate him, not that he became a hero by merely human decision.

Thucydides mentions several steps taken by the Amphipolitans to mark Brasidas' new status. The first, coming immediately after the burial, is the erection of a barrier *(perieirxantes)* around his memorial. This made the space into what is elsewhere called a *temenos,* a "place cut off," an area set aside for the cult of the god or hero worshiped within. Thenceforth this space formed a "hero-shrine"*(hêrôon),* and at least by the fourth century, perhaps as early as the fifth, such places combined the name of the hero with an adjectival termination signifying possession or connection, *-eion,* so that this one must have been a *Brasideion.*

Within this space the citizens sacrificed to Brasidas by the act of *entemnein,* a rare term that implies a method of slaughtering the victim so that the blood flowed "on" or "into" a certain place, perhaps the earth, as an ancient commentator explains, or perhaps the tomb itself. This is not a different rite from *enagizein,* "tabooing," which Herodotus used to describe the form of sacrifice made to Heracles "as to a hero." Rather, *entemnein* denotes the procedure whereby the sacrificer immolated the victim, while *enagizein* denotes the ceremony as a whole, and does not necessarily imply a sacrifice of blood.[7]

The cult of the hero always centered on his grave, and sometimes more than one city claimed to have his burial place, but the interment of the newly dead within a city's walls is exceptional: the Athenians, for instance, asserted that they had never granted the right of burial within the city to anyone. Elsewhere, this is normally a sign of heroic status, as for Battos of Cyrene, who like Brasidas was buried close to the agora.[8]

The Amphipolitans, in Thucydides' phrase, gave Brasidas "honors *(timas)* in the form of contests *(agônas)* and yearly sacrifices *(thusias)*." The word "honor" *(timê)* carries with it a notion of price or value, and often refers to something material or immaterial given as a mark of esteem. *Agôn,* as its connection with "agony" implies, means "contest, struggle," rather than "games," as it is often translated. Like burial within the city, periodic contests are not exclusive to heroes, but are very often a mark of heroization. The great literary precedent is the series of "contests" arranged by Achilles at the tomb of Patroclos, but a more immediate model was provided by the great contests of Greece centering on the tomb of a hero, as the Olympics centered on the tomb of Pelops, the settler from Asia Minor who gave his name to the Peloponnese.[9]

From the commemoration of Brasidas, Thucydides turns to what is in effect an act of reverse commemoration, the abolition of all marks of Hagnon, the original founder of the city, so that the citizens destroyed the "buildings connected with Hagnon" *(ta Hagnôneia oikodomêmata).* Some have understood this phrase to mean simply "public buildings of Hagnon," others "buildings named after Hagnon" as founder of the colony, while another view is that they are buildings for his worship; since Hagnon was probably still alive in 424, this has therefore been understood as an early reference to the cult of living heroes. It is true that buildings for the worship of a god or hero do have the termination *-eion,* for example, *Homêreion* for a temple of Homer, but the Greek suffix means no more than "belonging to," "associated with," so that Herodotus, for example, can talk of *Homêreia epê,* "Homeric verses," without any implication of cult. The heroization of a living person is a very rare phenomenon, and a founder would not be commemorated in several places of the city: Thucydides' only other use of the plural *oikodomêmata* refers to the several buildings, secular and religious, that the Athenians had built with moneys from the state treasury before the Peloponnesian War.[10]

The Amphipolitans made Brasidas their founder-hero because they considered him their "savior" *(sôtêr).* This term was to have a long history in cult, but does not need to imply divinity, and is sometimes no more than a polite way of addressing a superior. Nonetheless, it points to one of the essential ingredients of heroization as it was to develop over succeeding centuries: the notion of "benefaction" *(euergesia),* especially when manifested in acts that guaranteed the continuance of civic life, or gave such life a new beginning.[11]

The period of the Persian Wars in the first quarter of the fifth century appears to have brought about a new development in the commemoration of the war-dead, whereby they receive collective honors, as opposed to the commemoration of aristocratic founders such as Battos at Cyrene and Miltiades in the Chersonese. At the same time, the surviving texts are reluctant to use the word "hero" in these contexts, especially at Athens, and prefer to talk of the dead as enjoying a state of bliss in the underworld and to locate them towards the heroic end of a range of possible existences rather than making them into full heroes. Even after the battle of Marathon in 490, the Athenians buried their fallen in the usual Greek way on the battlefield itself, and there is no evidence that the full citizenry raised them to the status of heroes: by contrast, the demesmen of Marathon did so regard them, at least in the Roman period, telling stories about the sounds of battle that could still be heard at night and about the ghosts that could bring bad luck on those who met them. It has been proposed that the cavalcade of horsemen on the Parthenon frieze represents the heroized dead of Marathon, but this does not seem to accord with the Athenians' general reluctance to heroize their war-dead.[12]

After their defeat of the Persians at Plataea in 479, the combined Greek forces sacrificed to Zeus the Liberator *(Eleutherios)* in the Plataean agora. Diodorus Siculus and Plutarch, writing centuries later, provide detailed accounts of the subsequent comemorations, but it is doubtful whether these go back to the beginning. Both writers trace back to 479 the great Panhellenic contest called the *Eleutheria* (Games of Liberation), held like the Olympic and the Pythian games every fourth year, but more probably this began only in the period of Macedonian domination in the later fourth century.[13]

Separately from this Panhellenic celebration, the Plataeans instituted their own ceremony, which bears all the marks of a formal *enagismos,* at least in the form described by Plutarch, who may well have observed it personally. At daybreak a procession started from the city to the battle-field. Wagons carried wreaths of myrtle, a black bull was led out, and free-born youths brought offerings of wine, milk, oil, and myrrh; no slave could touch any of these objects, since the day celebrated men who had died for freedom. The chief magistrate, who on other days could not touch iron or wear any color other than white, advanced through the middle of the city to the site of the graves wearing a purple robe and carrying a sword. There he washed the tombs with water, anointed them with myrrh, slaughtered the bull "into" a funeral pyre, and "after praying to Zeus and Hermes of the Earth *(Chthonios)* [summoned] the brave men *(agathoi)* who died for Hellas to come to the banquet and the blood-offering *(haimakouria)*." Thereafter he mixed water and wine and poured a libation, saying, "I drink a toast to the men *(andres)* who died for the freedom of the Hellenes."[14]

From an uncertain date, the first attested one being 465/64, the Athenians began to bury their war-dead collectively in the burying-ground of the Kerameikos. A law that Thucydides calls "ancestral" *(patrios)* laid down rules for the funeral and interment of all the war-dead of a single year; at a later date there was added the rule that a leading statesman should pronounce the oration.[15] The best known of these speeches is the one delivered by Pericles in the first winter of the Peloponnesian War, known from its classic recasting by Thucydides. Of the other surviving examples, none are of certain authenticity except the latest, spoken by Hyperides in 322 over those who had fallen defending Greece against the Macedonian regent Antigonos.[16]

These later speeches share several themes. One is the perceived continuity between the legendary heroes and the newly dead. Several of the speakers adduce precedents for Athenian valor from the legendary past, such as Erechtheus in the war with Eleusis and the Athenians' protection of the descendants of Heracles. Yet while these orators extol the happy lot of the fallen in the next world, their superior status, and their resemblance to the ancient heroes, they refrain from calling them by that name (though the word is sometimes introduced by modern translators). Thus Lysias in his speech for the dead of the Corinthian War: "They are mourned because of their nature as mortals *(thnêtoi)*, but hymned as immortals *(athanatoi)* because of their virtue. For they are buried at public expense, and in their honor contests of strength, wisdom, and wealth are conducted, on the ground that those who have died in war deserve to be honored with the same honors as the immortals *(hoi athanatoi)*." So also Demosthenes, or a later writer posing as him, claims that the glorious deeds of the Athenians in heroic time are the stuff of poetry, while the deeds of their present successors "have not yet been turned into myth or raised to the station of the heroes." We should think of the recently dead as "sitting beside the gods below, having the same station as the brave men *(agathoi andres)* in the Islands of the Blest," where they are no doubt as much honored as they are on earth.[17]

The last of these speeches, that of Hyperides, has in its background both those recently fallen in the Lamian War after Alexander's death and Alexander's own heroization of Hephaestion, his comrade-in-arms and closest friend, in 324. According to some ancient sources, Alexander had asked the oracle of Ammon if Hephaestion might receive "sacrifice as for a god" *(hôs theô thuein)*, and been rebuffed, whereupon he issued a general order for "the hero Hephaestion" to receive *enagismos* forever. In response, Athens set up a joint cult of Alexander as a god and of Hephaestion as his companion *(parhedros)* in the following winter.[18]

Hyperides delivered his funeral oration a year or so later, when the consequences of Antigonos' defeat of the Greeks had not yet become clear, and as a staunch opponent of Macedon he was not likely to be sympathetic to treating Alexander and his companion as having a status more than human. Even so, the distinction that he draws between Hephaestion, heroized by official demand, and the patriotic dead, close to the ancient heroes but not their equals, follows the tradition of Athenian public oratory. "We might well reflect what in our opinion the outcome would have been, had these men failed to do their duty in the struggle . . . The practices which even now we have to countenance are proof enough; sacrifices being made to human beings; images *(agalmata)*, altars, and temples carefully perfected in their honor, while those of the gods are neglected, and we ourselves are forced to honor as heroes the slaves *(oiketas)* of these people." By contrast, the fallen have not died, but have entered on a new existence in Hades. "Who, we may well ask ourselves, are waiting there to welcome the leader of these men? Are we not convinced that we would see, greeting Leosthenes with wonder, those of the so-called demigods who sailed against Troy, men whose deeds he so far excelled, though his exploits were akin to theirs? . . . Those too, I think, who gave the people the surest token of their mutual friendship, Harmodius and Aristogiton, do not regard any men as closer to themselves than Leosthenes and his comrades in arms; nor are there any with whom they would rather hold converse in the lower world than these."[19]

A discovery on Thasos in the northern Aegean in the 1950s produced a new example of collective heroization in a city other than Athens, but here too the word "hero" is avoided. A decree dated to the mid-fourth century records honors for "the Brave" *(hoi Agathoi)*, men recently fallen in some conflict no longer identifiable. The citizens are not to mourn the dead for more than five days, nor to hold private funerals for them. The city is to inscribe their names and will also invite their fathers and sons "when it makes sacrifice *(entemnein)* to the Brave." The rare verb *entemnein*, also used by Thucydides for Brasidas at Amphipolis, may imply that the Thasians regarded these war-dead as heroes, but could imply some position in the next world near but not equal to the heroes of old.[20]

With the decline of the city as a major player in Greek politics, and the rise of confederated states and kingdoms, the need arose for politicians who could steer their communities through the fluctuations caused by rivalries between higher powers. An early example is Euphron of Sicyon in the northeastern Peloponnese. In 371 the Theban defeat of the Spartans at the battle of Leuctra ended Sparta as a major power and led to a series of realignments within the Peloponnese, as the oligarchic regimes favored by Sparta yielded to democratic ones and new entities such as the Arcadian league came into being. In 368 or 366, Euphron, a wealthy citizen of Sicyon who had hitherto been pro-Spartan, brought his city over to the Thebans. These allowed him to create a radical democracy, in which he freed slaves, exiled his oligarchic opponents, and raised a large mercenary force that he controlled by putting his son in command. The surviving accounts, notably that of the pro-Spartan Xenophon, represent him as a "tyrant" or a "madman," but he enjoyed great popularity in Sicyon both in his lifetime and after death. Towards the end of his life, the restored oligarchy banished him from the city and he fled to Thebes, where he was murdered. The Thebans acquitted his killers, but "his own citizens . . . , esteeming him a good man, brought him home, buried him in the market place, and revere *(sebontai)* him as the first founder *(archêgetês)* of their city. So true it is, it seems, that most people define their own benefactors as good men *(andras agathous)*." Though Xenophon does not use the term "hero," Euphron's burial in the agora, and his veneration as an *archêgetês*, make it likely that he was so regarded.[21]

"Great Greece" *(megalê Hellas, Magna Graecia)*, the western extension of Greece in Sicily and southern Italy, developed in different political directions from the motherland, and "tyranny," the rule of unelected and hereditary autocrats, struck deeper roots there. In 344 the citizens of Syracuse, then under the "tyranny" of Dionysios II, appealed to the mother-city Corinth for help. Corinth sent out Timoleon, who deposed Dionysios, established a democracy in Syracuse, though he himself was supreme military commander *(stratêgos autokratôr)* for eight continuous years, and then proceeded to eject "tyrants" and establish "democracy" in many cities of eastern Sicily, which he repopulated from all over Greece. At the same time, his campaigns against the Carthaginians in the western part of the island allowed a revived Hellenism to flourish. After his death in the later 330s, the Syracusans cremated his body, buried his ashes in the agora, and resolved to hold games in perpetuity in his memory. He is the first "new hero" known to have received a monument named in his honor, the *Timoleonteion;* this had an adjacent gymnasium for the use of the city's youth, and the combination of heroic memorial and gymnasium was to become more frequent in later centuries.[22]

The favorable treatment that Timoleon receives in the extant sources goes back to the third century Sicilian historian, Timaeus of Tauromenium (Taormina). In the following century, Polybius is fiercely critical of Timaeus' treatment, sarcastically comparing Sicily, the sphere of Timoleon's heroics, to a "saucer." "Timaeus makes Timoleon greater than the most manifest gods . . . As it seems to me, he was convinced that if Timoleon, who had won glory in Sicily as if in a saucer, were to seem comparable to the most manifest of the heroes, he himself by writing merely about Italy and Sicily might be thought comparable to those authors whose works concerned the world and general events." These criticisms reveal Polybius' own pride in his wide historical perspective and his dislike of the irrational in history, but in his aversion to hero-worship he is behind his times.[23]

In the Greek heartland and in Asia Minor, first Macedon under Philip and Alexander, and then the Successor Kingdoms after the dissolution of the Macedonian Empire became the dominant powers and brought about many changes in Greek society. Leading citizens could still be honored as heroes, as Euphron was at Sicyon, but now their honors are due to their diplomacy and their ability to steer the cities or their confederations in times of shifting alliances and wars between states. The kings who rule such states can demand heroic status for their favorites, or cities may grant such status to win their approval. From about the year 200, as Rome advances further and further into the Greek world, "heroes" tend more and more to be statesmen who have guided their communities in pro-Roman directions, or at least these are the ones whose monuments survive.

The traveler Pausanias notes that on the territory of Daulis in southeastern Phocis there was a shrine of an unnamed "founder hero" (*hêrôs archêgetês*), and he comments: "This founder is said by some to have been Xanthippos, a distinguished soldier; others say that he was Phocos, son of Ornytion, son of Sisyphos. At any rate, he is worshipped every day, and the Phocians bring victims and pour the blood into the grave through a hole, but the flesh they are wont to consume on the spot." Thus by the author's time, either because the monument had never named the founder or because the inscription had become illegible over time, he had to rely on local guides who identified the person commemorated either as the eponymous hero of the region, Phocos, or as a dimly remembered Xanthippos.[24]

This Xanthippos, whose name meant so little to Pausanias, was a mere shadow until inscriptions of Delphi revealed his importance. When Cassander the king of Macedon was besieging the important Phocian city of Elatea in the year 301, Xanthippos as general of the Phocians, together with the general and statesman Olympiodoros of Athens, led the forces that lifted the siege. Some fifteen years later, when the new king Antigonos Gonatas had installed a garrison in Elatea, Xanthippos again managed to liberate the city and to free Phocis. The league thereafter set up two statues in his honor at Delphi, of which the second ends thus: "For these reasons, stranger, ten times did the Phocians choose Xanthippos as general, and all called blessings on him with their praise. When a person looks on Xanthippos, the son of Ampharatos, let him say; 'See how great are the thanks paid to the good.'" "Thanks paid to the good" recalls Xenophon's comment on the heroization of Euphron of Sicyon, "So true it is, as it seems, that most people define their own benefactors as good men," and suggests that the Phocians had successfully applied to Apollo of Delphi to inquire if they might honor Xanthippos as a hero. To judge by the intensity of the cult in Pausanias' day, the personality of Xanthippos had merged with that of the local eponym, Phocos. This may have been a development of the Roman period in which cities refurbished their mythical ancestry in order to justify their claims of antiquity.[25]

Two other statesmen, one of the late third century and the other of the early second, exemplify the narrowing scope for heroism on the part of notable Greeks in the Hellenistic period, who like Xanthippos acted less as civilian leaders of their communities than as generals of confederations or "leagues" *(koina)*. The first of these, Aratus, is from Euphron's city of Sicyon. Only moderately successful as a general in the field, Aratus nonetheless managed, by means of force, craft, and abrupt changes of policy, to bring Sicyon into the Peloponnesian alliance called the Achaean League and to build the League into a major power in the politics of the later third century. In the year 213, he died at the age of fifty-seven, allegedly poisoned by the Macedonian king Philip V. According to Plutarch, the League wished to bury him in Aegium where he had died, but his fellow-citizens claimed his remains, wishing to bury him within their walls, where an ancient law, strongly reinforced by popular belief, forbade the burial of humans. They applied to Apollo of Delphi, the usual source of authority for religious innovation, and on obtaining a positive answer changed from black clothing into white, escorted the body into the city, and buried it in a conspicuous place, henceforth named the *Arateion*. As a founder and savior, Aratus was honored with two separate festivals of sacrifice. One, the *Sotêria* or "Festival of Salvation," commemorated his youthful exploit in freeing Sicyon from tyranny, and the priest of Zeus the Savior *(Zeus Sôtêr)* presided over the rites. The other was held on his birthday, and here a priest of Aratus presided, the earliest instance of a "new hero" having his own priest. As a moralist, Plutarch is uncomfortable with man-made divinities and in his biography of Aratus does not call him a hero, while Pausanias refers to his burial place as a *hêrôon* and says that the Sicyonians considered him to be the son of Asclepius. Like the assimilation of Xanthippos to the hero Phocos, this may represent a later attempt to lift a long-dead hero out of the purely human sphere and to make him a "demigod" *(hêmitheos)* like the heroes of epic.[26]

The other great Achaean statesman, and the successor of Aratus, was Philopoemen of Megalopolis, whose policy of maintaining Greek independence often brought him into conflict with the encroaching power of Rome. A Roman called him "the last of the Greeks," and he is the last Greek to be included by Plutarch in the *Parallel Lives.* At the end of his account, Plutarch describes how the Messenians, hereditary enemies of the Arcadians, captured and poisoned Philopoemen, whereupon the Arcadians in revenge ravaged Messenia, forced the Messenians to come to terms, and then brought his remains back to Megalopolis with elaborate ceremony. As with Aratus, Plutarch dwells on the details of Philopoemen's death and burial. A troop of soldiers escorted the body home more in triumph than in mourning, the urn carrying the ashes was decorated with ribbons, and along the way people poured out of towns and villages to touch it and accompany it back to Megalopolis. There the citizens buried Philopoemen "gloriously" *(endoxôs)* and stoned their Messenian captives around the tomb. Again as with Aratus, Plutarch is glossing over an act of official heroization, since another source, Diodorus Siculus, says that the city granted him "godlike honors" *(isotheoi timai),* including an altar, annual sacrifice, and hymns sung by a chorus of youths. A fragmentary inscription shows further that the city associated him with Zeus the Savior, as Sicyon had done for Aratus, and that he received a sanctuary *(temenos),* sacrifices, and periodic contests *(agônes).*[27]

Despite the death of the "last of the Greeks," Hellenism had centuries of history before it, though henceforth the action of Greek patriots is more and more tied to the fortunes of Rome. Those who receive heroic honors may be men who fall on the battlefield, but they do so in the service of Rome; they may also be men whose influence with great Romans enables them to "save" their cities in novel ways, by deprecating the anger of the dominant power or steering their cities across the shoals of civil war. One such is Apollonios son of Attalos from the little city of Metropolis in Ionia. A long decree has revealed him as an ardent supporter of Rome in the troubled years after the last king of Pergamum, Attalus III, died leaving his realm to the Romans. Aristonicos, a self-proclaimed half-brother of the late king, raised an army and tried to seize the throne, and in the ensuing "War of Aristonicos," Apollonios fell while leading a contingent from his city. Before his body had been recovered and the bones brought home, the citizens passed a long decree that among other provisions permitted his sons to build a *hêrôon* for him before the city-gate on their own property. The detail, "on their own property," reveals a new modification in the nature of heroic honors. The *hêrôon* is not on a public site such as the agora (though such public burial continues to occur for several centuries) but on private land; there is thus a convergence between the public heroization of the classical and Hellenistic periods and the personal heroization that is so marked in the period of the Roman Empire.[28]

The last generations of the Roman republic introduced new complications into the life of the Greek city. Now the choice was not always between Rome and another power, as it had been as recently as the Roman wars against Mithridates VI of Pontus, but between rival parties within Rome itself. A decree of Cyzicus, carved on a now-lost stone, reveals the fortunes of three generations of the same family. The grandfather and patriarch is a certain Asclepiades, called the "founder *(oikistês),"* who had received from the grateful citizens annual "heroic contests" *(agônes hêrôoi)* celebrated in gratitude to him and "those who fought with him at Alexandria in the war against Ptolemy." This is the "Alexandrian War" in which Julius Caesar, pursuing Pompey to Egypt, became embroiled in dynastic struggles between Cleopatra VII and her brother Ptolemy XIII, and found his retreat from Alexandria cut off. He owed his rescue to reinforcements sent by nearby allies, who included an eminent citizen of Pergamon, Mithridates. In the next generation Asclepiades' son or son-in-law, Oeniades, was honored with an annual parade *(katadromê)*. The decree itself honors Asclepiades' grandson Demetrios, probably in the reign of Augustus. He is to receive a crown at the games in honor of Rome *(Rhômaia)*, and a second one at the contests in honor of his grandfather, a tondo portrait on a gilded shield, and a "cult-statue of marble" *(agalma marmarinon)* in the sanctuary of Apollo and Asclepius. In addition, the parade established for Oeniades will in future start from the *hêrôon* and end at a stoa currently being constructed by his brother Dionysios.[29]

This document, mutilated as it is, attests to the vitality of the heroic tradition in the last decades of the republic, and at the same time to its

evolution. The grandfather, Asclepiades, is a "founder" *(oikistês)*, as Miltiades the Elder was a "founder" in the sixth-century Chersonese. Five centuries on, *oikistês* had become synonymous with the word that properly
implies the foundation of a building, *ktistês,* and Asclepiades receives his
title because the help he had given to Caesar brought privileges to Cyzicus that in effect gave it a second birth. His contemporary and fellow-
soldier in the Alexandrian campaign, Mithridates of Pergamon, who by
helping Caesar on the same occasion secured several advantages for his
city, provides a close parallel. Pergamon recovered the liberty it had lost
in the time of Sulla, and an inscription honors Mithridates for "having
restored the city and the territory to the ancestral gods, and becoming a
new founder *(ktistês)* of his city after Pergamos and Philetairos" (Pergamos is the legendary founder, Philetairos the ancestor of the Attalid
line of kings). Asclepiades too must have obtained benefits for Cyzicus
that made him a hero to his citizens, a second Cyzicus as Mithridates
was a second Pergamos and Philetairos. Probably his "heroic honors"
were voted in his lifetime in anticipation of his death, and the next generations of the family maintained the tradition of benefaction and were
buried in the same shrine.[30]

Unlike Asclepiades, other Greeks active in the last decades of the Roman republic usually become Roman citizens, and take the family
names of the protagonists of the civil wars, "Pompeius," "Antonius," but
above all "Julius," whether their patron was the dictator or his adopted
son, the later Augustus. One such who links the end of the Republic
with the beginning of the Principate is Gaius Julius Zoilus from Aphrodisias in Caria. Zoilus was a freedman of either the elder or the younger
Caesar, perhaps a freed captive rather than a slave by birth. Exactly
when he began his career is not known, but he served his city in the tur-
bulent decade of the 30s, when the Roman renegade Labienus led Persian forces deep into southern Asia Minor, and the rivalry between
Antony and Octavian hardened into outright war. At the same time
Zoilus contributed to major building projects of the city, of which the
most visible now is the stage building of the excellently preserved the-
ater. In addition, an architrave of the city's chief sanctuary, the Temple
of Aphrodite, calls him "savior and benefactor of his native city" *(sôtêr
kai euergetês tês patridos)*. Before or after his death, the citizens voted

Zoilus an elaborate funeral monument that almost certainly served as a heroic shrine *(hêrôon)*, perhaps known as the *Zoileion*. The base of this was surrounded by panels of which several survive, and these give a vivid idea of the concept of the warrior-hero in this last stage of its development. The figures represented include Eternity *(Aiôn)*, Rome, the City, the People, and Courage *(Andreia)*. Another panel shows Minos, one of the judges of the dead in the underworld; Zoilus was perhaps represented standing before him, waiting to receive a favorable verdict and to dwell with the heroes in the next life.[31]

Zoilus' title of "savior and benefactor" encapsulates the convergence of salvation and benefaction that can be traced back at least as far as Brasidas at Amphipolis. Yet the fact that both Rome and Minos appear on Zoilus' tomb shows that old conceptions had become fused with more modern ones. These citizens who aided the Romans in the civil wars often became the founders of a new aristocracy in the Greek city of the Roman Empire. One such is Gaius Julius Eurycles of Sparta, whom a contemporary descended from Brasidas mocked as a *parvenu;* after his death Eurycles was honored with contests called *Eurycleia,* and one of his descendants in the second century claimed to trace his ancestry back to Castor and Pollux, the sons of Zeus and Leda.[32] Military heroism is rarely open to the Greek citizen of the Roman imperial period, though the barbarian invasions of the second and third centuries were to give it renewed scope.[33] Notwithstanding, heroes and heroines of other kinds continue to arise and to find their worshipers.

CHAPTER 4

Athletes, Poets, Philosophers

✦

In a fragment of a poem now lost, Pindar declares that Persephone, the queen of the underworld, allows the souls of certain exceptional men to return "to the upper sunlight," and that from these souls "arise proud kings and men who are swift in strength and greatest in wisdom, and for the rest of time people call them sacred heroes."[1] By extending the word "hero" to cover men of exceptional endowment, physical and intellectual, Pindar gives it a meaning markedly different from the Homer of the *Iliad* and Hesiod, though the poet of the *Odyssey* had already given the title to the wise king Alcinoos and the bard Demodocos.

Until the end of the Hellenistic period, when war ceased to be part of the daily life of the ordinary Greek citizen, death in battle continued to be the prime avenue to heroic status, a conjunction reinforced by admiration for the poems of Homer and Hesiod. But "men who are swift in strength and greatest in wisdom" also receive cult of various kinds, even if they do not always earn the status of heroes. These are athletes, poets, and philosophers.

Several athletes of archaic and classical Greece became the theme of miraculous stories about their strength, their power to do good as well as evil, and their curious fates after death. Of these the mysterious Oebatas of Dyme in Achaea, the alleged winner in the foot-race at Olympia in 756, is the earliest in time. Resentful because the Achaeans did not honor him for his victory, he cursed them and, in the words of Pausanias, "since there was one of the gods who was concerned that the curses of Oebatas be fulfilled," for centuries no Achaean won an Olympic victory. After consulting Delphi and learning the reason, the Achaeans set up a statue for him in the shrine, and thereafter began to win again. "Even in my day," observes Pausanias, "it remains the custom that those Achaeans planning to compete in the Olympics make funerary offerings *(enagizein)* to Oebatas." Here as elsewhere there appears the idea that an Olympic victor must necessarily enjoy divine favor, and that to dishonor him is to run the risk of retribution.[2]

A closely similar story concerns another Olympic victor from Italian Locri, a winner in the pentathlon called Euthycles whose history entered into the *Aetia* of the poet Callimachus. After serving as an ambassador for his city, on his return home Euthycles was accused of accepting bribes and died in prison. In retaliation for his alleged crime, the Locrians mutilated his statues and were subsequently struck with famine. They consulted Apollo of Delphi, and received an oracle of which the sense appears to have been that athletes had the special favor of the gods. They then set up a cult-statue *(agalma)* of Euthycles and an altar on which they thereafter sacrificed to him on a fixed day. How much historical fact lies behind these stories is now irrecoverable: more important is the recurrence of certain motifs, the protection of the dead athlete by watchful gods and his propitiation by means of sacrifice before his statue.[3]

A more complicated case is that of Euthymos, a thrice Olympic victor also from Italian Locri. From the list of Olympic victors he is known to have won several victories in boxing in the early fifth century. According to a tradition that again goes back to the poet Callimachus, Euthymos freed his city from a "hero" who had once been a member of Odysseus' crew and after death had exacted a periodic tribute *(dasmos)* from the locals by taking the virginity of their daughters. Callimachus' account survives only in a prose summary by the Elder Pliny, and if correctly quoted the poet said that Euthymos was "consecrated while still living and sentient" and received sacrifice "both alive and dead." Visiting Olympia a century after Pliny, Pausanias heard a more elaborate version of Euthymos and his fight with the hero, in which Euthymos himself was the son of a local river and escaped death by some process that the author does not describe. (The base of his statue at

Olympia, with the inscription read by Pausanias, still survives.) Like Oebatas and Euthycles, Euthymos is of interest for the aura that surrounded Olympic victors and for the tales that grew up about them and their statues in their home towns and in the great sanctuaries of Greece; but the accounts of his exploits are too late and too embroidered to make him a convincing example of a new hero.[4]

Once in his career Euthymos was defeated by Theogenes or (to use the later form of his name) Theagenes of Thasos, one of the greatest of "heavy" athletes of antiquity, whose phenomenal feats of strength from an early age caused him to be thought the son of Heracles, the patron-hero of athletes. Theagenes' extraordinary career brought him over a thousand victories as a boxer and pancratiast, though he once competed as a long-distance runner in Pharsalos, the successor-city to the Homeric Phthia; Pausanias inferred that he had chosen to compete here because it was the home of the "swift-footed" Achilles. The Periegete proceeds to give a long account of Theagenes that has much in common with his account of Euthymos of Locri. His fellow-citizens set up a statue of him in their agora, which after his death one of his enemies whipped mercilessly until one day it fell and killed him. The Thasians then put the statue on trial for homicide, condemned it, and threw it into the sea. When they began to suffer a series of bad harvests, they turned to Apollo of Delphi to learn the cause and were told to "restore those they had driven out." When they realized that the god referred to the statue, they were at a loss what to do until fishermen found it entangled in their nets, whereupon they set it up again in their agora, and in Pausanias' time still sacrificed to Theagenes as to a god. "There are many other places that I know of," continues the traveler, "both among Greeks and barbarians, where sacred images *(agalmata)* of Theagenes have been set up, and he cures diseases and receives honors from the locals."[5] Discoveries on Thasos have confirmed many of these statements, though as yet there is no archaeological evidence for his worship elsewhere. Already by the late Hellenistic period he receives cult as a god *(theos)*, and from the first century C.E. onwards, he is an "ancestral" *(patrios)* or "manifest" *(epiphanês)* god. Like other of these early athletes, Theagenes is not called a hero, but his apotheosis is another eloquent reminder of the aura surrounding these men of huge physical strength.[6]

The most famous and mysterious of these superhuman athletes is Cleomedes of Astypalaea, who killed his opponent in boxing at the Olympics of 492 and was deprived of his victory. Driven mad by resentment, after his return home he pulled down the supporting column of a school and killed the sixty children inside. The enraged citizens chased him into a sanctuary of Athena, where he climbed into a chest and pulled down the lid. Finding themselves mysteriously powerless to remove the lid, his pursuers broke the chest open at the sides, only to find it empty. They sent an inquiry to Delphi, which replied:

> Latest of the heroes is Cleomedes the Astypalaean;
> Honor him with sacrifices as one no longer mortal.

"So from this time," observes Pausanias, "the Astypalaeans have paid honor to Cleomedes as to a hero." This story interested Plutarch as a parallel to the disappearance of Romulus, and Christian authors because of its seeming similarities to the empty tomb of Jesus. It is perhaps because of the exceptional nature of Cleomedes' disappearance that he is the only one of these fabled athletes to be unambiguously called a hero.[7]

These early athletes, most of them grouped in the first part of the fifth century, are marginal to the study of new heroes. They are closer to the minor divinities known sometimes as heroes, at other times as spirits (*daimones*), who are jealous of their prerogatives and quick to punish offenders, as, for example, the *Anagyrasios daimôn*, hero of the deme Anagyrasioi in Attica, who punished a man for cutting down his sacred grove by killing him, his son, and his mistress. In later times, athletes who die young may receive posthumous honors from their fellow-athletes or fellow-citizens, but if they become heroes, they are not credited with any special powers for good or ill.[8]

When Odysseus has slain the suitors, the minstrel Phemios pleads for his life. "By your knees I beseech you, Odysseus, and do you respect me and have pity; on your own self shall sorrow come hereafter, if you kill the minstrel, me, who sing to gods and men. I am self-taught, and the god has planted in my heart lays of all sorts, and worthy am I to sing to you as to a god; therefore do not be eager to cut my throat." Phemios' speech takes for granted the close affinity between poets and gods, and his threat that Odysseus will suffer for harming him is an implicit claim of divine favor, recalling the gods who intervened to fulfill the curses of athletes such as Oebatas. In later literature poets, above all Homer, are often called *theioi*, "divine," a term that does not impute divinity to them, but rather extraordinary attributes that can only come from the especial favor of the gods.[9]

An isolated quotation from Alcidamas, a teacher of rhetoric approximately contemporary with Plato, concerns the honors paid to those who are *sophoi*, a word often translated "wise" but often applied to poets in the sense of "skilled." His examples are three poets and three "wise" men in the more usual sense of "thinkers" or "philosophers." Of his poets, he says: "The citizens of Paros have honored Archilochos despite his malice, and those of Chios Homer, though he was not a citizen; the Mityleneans have honored Sappho, though she was a woman." The verb "honor" *(timan)* is related to the noun *timê* that Thucydides uses for the heroic honors paid to Brasidas, and all three of the poets mentioned by Alcidamas received some form of cult.[10]

In Greek usage, Homer is the "divine poet" par excellence. Chios' claim to be his home, if not his birthplace, rested on the *Hymn to Apollo,* whose author calls himself "a blind man, (who) lives in rugged Chios." In the Hellenistic period, the Chiotes had a "Homeric Gymnasium" *(Homêreion gymnasion);* by this period gymnasia were used not only for athletics but also for education, and like the *Timoleonteion* of Syracuse this one could have combined the functions of a cult-place and a school. The work called the *Contest of Homer and Hesiod,* which in its present form is not earlier than the reign of Hadrian, states that the Argives voted to sacrifice in the poet's honor at Chios every fourth year, so that there may have been a local festival named for him. In the fourth century, the emperor Julian mentions a Delphic oracle that called Homer a "hero and spirit" *(hêrôs kai daimôn),* but in what context it did so is unknown.[11]

Smyrna, though mentioned neither by Homer nor by Alcidamas, was the city most usually taken to be his birthplace, a claim as old as the fifth century. Smyrnaean coins of the later Hellenistic period show the poet seated with a book on his knees and a scepter symbolizing his kingly supremacy among poets. In his defense of the poet Archias, Cicero names several cities that claimed to be Homer's birthplace, but singles out Smyrna for having a temple *(delubrum)* dedicated to him. This *Homêreion* was a quadrangular portico enclosing a temple *(neôs)* and an image *(xoanon)* of Homer, a term implying an image hieratic in form, though not necessarily ancient. The word *neôs* or *naos* is related to the verb *naiô*, "dwell," and designates some building or part of a building within which a god or hero resided. If the oracle quoted by Julian can be trusted, and Homer was worshiped as a hero, Smyrna may well have been the center of his cult.[12]

Alexandria in Egypt could not claim to be Homer's birthplace, though legend said that he advised Alexander where to found it. This too had a celebrated *Homêreion,* a temple *(neôs)* built by Ptolemy Philopator, a great patron of learning and a poet himself. A fragmentary epigram asserts that Ptolemy had been ordered in a dream to build the sanctuary *(temenos)* "for Homer, who once wrote the ageless poems of the *Odyssey* and the *Iliad* from his immortal mind." In the sanctuary, Homer's cult-statue *(agalma)* represented him enthroned and surrounded by personifications of the cities that claimed his birth.[13]

A celebrated work of Hellenistic art, probably of the second century, is the so-called *Apotheosis of Homer* by the sculptor Archelaos of Priene. This does not in fact represent the poet as he undergoes apotheosis, but as he receives veneration from various gods and allegorical figures. In the top register sits Zeus, turning towards Memory *(Mnêmosynê)*, while their nine daughters, the Muses, occupy the two registers below. In the bottom one, the poet sits holding a staff within what appears to be a sanctuary, while his "daughters," the personified *Iliad* and the *Odyssey,* crouch at his feet. The World *(Oikoumenê)* and Time *(Chronos)* crown him, and before him is an altar on which Myth and History sacrifice a bull. A later work of art, a cup found at Pompeii, has a better title to be called an "apotheosis," since it shows the poet being carried heavenward by an eagle, while the personified *Iliad* and *Odyssey* mourn his departure from among mankind.[14]

Hesiod, sometimes regarded as a contemporary and rival of Homer, became the subject of several miraculous tales that suggest a form of heroization. He himself claims to have met the Muses while tending his sheep in a valley beneath Mount Helicon, and pays them glowing tribute in the opening of his *Theogony*. This valley contained a sanctuary for their cult *(Mouseion)*, and in the Hellenistic period an association called "the Hesiodic co-sacrificers *(synthytai)* to the Muses" owned property nearby. This is probably a poetic guild that used the site for its meetings and celebrated the memory of Hesiod, but not a group worshiping the poet himself. Similarly the Platonists of Athens met to sacrifice, probably to Apollo, on the birthdays of Socrates and Plato; at Miletus there were *Timotheastai* and *Hegesiastai,* associations devoted to the lyric poet Timotheos and the historian Hegesias, and not necessarily cult-groups. So also when the poet Statius cultivated the tomb of Vergil as a *templum,* this need not imply more than professional reverence for his great predecessor's resting place.[15]

Sappho from Eresos on Lesbos was acclaimed as "the tenth Muse" and as the equal of Homer among women poets, and her fame lasted into Late Antiquity, with the papyri showing a peak of interest in the second and third centuries. On some Mytilenaean coins of the imperial period, she appears seated and playing the lyre, while in others she sits on a throne within a tetrastyle temple. Here too, therefore, like Homer at Smyrna and Alexandria, she must have enjoyed some form of cult. At the small city of Olympos in southeastern Lycia in the second or third century, a certain Aurelius Chariton has the extra name of "Sapphodoros," "Sappho's Gift." Names of this form usually designate the bearer as the gift of a god or goddess, less often of a hero or a river. Chariton's first name links him with the Graces *(Charites),* and "Sapphodoros" suggests that he was in some way blessed by Sappho, perhaps because his parents had prayed to her before his birth, or because his poetic accomplishments were her "gift."[16]

In his list of "wise" persons receiving posthumous "honor," Alcidamas began with the poet Archilochos on Paros, and archaeology has fully confirmed his testimony. Already by the year 500, the Parians had a monument that showed the poet as a warrior, reclining and drinking, with a shield hanging on the wall above him; this relief may have formed part of a *peribolos* or sanctuary wall. In the early fourth century, one Dokimos set up a monument *(mnêmeion)* over the poet's grave, perhaps in the form of an archaic sphinx. About a hundred years later, a certain Mnesiepes established an enclosed sanctuary *(temenos)* in his honor, and about a hundred years after him, one Sositheos enlarged the site by consecrating Archilochos' portrait and setting up a new account of his life, drawn from an otherwise unknown Demeas. This tells how Mnesiepes had approached Delphic Apollo for approval of his plan and received three oracles in reply. The first two named the gods to whom he was to sacrifice, principally the Muses, Apollo the "leader of the Muses" *(Mousagetês),* and Memory; in the third response, Apollo encouraged Mnesiepes' plan to "honor" Archilochos. Hence, says Sositheos' account, "we call the place the *Archilocheion,* and we set up the altars, sacrifice to the gods and to Archilochos, and honor him as the god bade us." The text proceeds to narrate Archilochos' early life. Going along a deserted country road, he met nine women who were in fact the Muses, though he did not recognize them; in return for the cow that he was leading, they gave him a lyre. (The story resembles Hesiod's meeting with the Muses on Helicon.) Later, his father consulted Delphi and received an oracle promising that his son would be "immortal and famous." In this form the *Archilocheion,* with its archaic portrait of the poet and its miraculous account of his life, appears to have lasted to the end of antiquity.[17]

The traditions concerning Sophocles are tangled. The third-century historian Ister is quoted as saying that the Athenians "voted to sacrifice to him yearly because of his virtue *(aretê)."* Medieval lexica are more circumstantial, saying that he was named "Dexion" after his death because "the Athenians, wanting to secure honors for Sophocles when he had died, provided a *hêrôon* for him and named him Dexion because of his reception *(dexis)* of Asclepius, since he received the god in his house and set up an altar." Though the medieval version is probably false, Ister's statement could be true. Much as the Amphipolitans passed a law ordaining sacrifice to Brasidas, so also the Athenians could have acknowledged the heroic status of Sophocles after his death, perhaps because of his close connection with Asclepius, in whose honor he wrote a celebrated paean. He had also served the Athenian state as a magistrate and a general.[18]

Alcidamas' list of *sophoi* contained three wise men as well as three poets. "The Spartans made Chilon one of their Elders, though they are not at all scholarly *(philologoi);* the Italians buried Pythagoras and honor him even now, although he was a stranger *(xenos);* and the Lampsacenes have done the same for Anaxagoras." Of these, Chilon's name, as already mentioned, appears on one of the early "hero-reliefs" of Sparta, and Pausanias saw his *hêrôon* there. Nothing seems to be known of a cult of Pythagoras in Italy, though one could certainly have existed among his Italian followers. His native Samos displays his bust on coins of the Hellenistic and imperial periods, as Lampsacos does for Anaxagoras, but neither of them is shown within a temple. Bias of Priene, the sixth-century philosopher who, like Chilon, was later counted as one of the Seven Wise Men of Greece, is said by a late source to have received a sanctuary *(temenos)* called the *Teutameion,* oddly named after his father Teutamos and not after himself. Inscriptions of Priene show that by the first century B.C.E., Priene had a sacred building called the *Bianteion,* which must have served for his cult. In general, it is remarkable how little evidence there is for the philosophers of the archaic period receiving veneration as heroes: at most they seem to receive a cult that places them on a higher level than the ordinary dead, but not with warriors and statesmen such as Brasidas and Timoleon.[19]

A philosopher of the imperial period forms a paradoxical exception, the Pythagorean Apollonius of Tyana. His youthful stay in the shrine of Asclepius at Aegeae in Cilicia was written up by one of the imperial secretaries; the emperor Hadrian collected Apollonius' letters; and Julia Domna, the consort of Septimius Severus, encouraged Philostratus of Athens to compose Apollonius' biography; Domna's son Caracalla built what Cassius Dio calls a *hêrôon* to Apollonius in Tyana. For Philostratus, he "surpassed human nature in wisdom"; an oracle of Apollo places him on a level with Egyptian Hermes and "Moses of the Hebrews"; and for fourth-century pagans he is "mid-way between the gods and a human." He was to prove the most durable of "divine" men of antiquity, and belief in his powers lasted well into the Middle Ages, even in the Christian Empire ruled from Constantinople.[20]

If Apollonius indeed became a new hero, he is one of the last. An inscription dated to 242, and so in the lifetime of Philostratus, is similarly the last record of a citizen honored as a hero, and he too is not one of the traditional kind but "a holy and honorable man *(hieros kai euprepês anêr)*." While the concept of the hero as a man of action and the belief in the heroes of myth were far from dead, long before the third century moral virtue *(aretê)* had become paramount in the conception of the heroic, allowing family members and civic benefactors, women as well as men, to become heroines and heroes of a new kind.[21]

CHAPTER 5

Private Heroes

.✦.

The warrior-hero of early epic and the patriotic heroes of the archaic and classical city—the collective dead such as the Greeks who fell at Marathon, pioneers such as Battos of Cyrene, saviors such as Brasidas—all these have in common the risking and sometimes the loss of their lives in war or for the good of their compatriots. At least to the end of the Hellenistic period, cities still heroize their war-dead, but as early as the fourth century there begins a new trend in which individuals can declare a person, or even themselves, a hero, with no suggestion of military prowess.

This trend is a development from the cult of local heroes who were the supposed ancestors of a prominent family or a whole community, such as Boutes the local hero of the deme Boutadae at Athens, and the rituals and iconography of such local heroes closely resemble those of private ones. Thus a relief of the early Hellenistic period shows a bearded man, "the hero Kydrogenes," reclining at a banquet, while a group of votaries, one of them also named Kydrogenes, cluster on either side of him with their arms raised in a gesture of adoration; behind him can be seen, in small window-like apertures, a shield, a horse's head, and three busts of women, again in the posture of adorants. In such cases it is often impossible to tell whether the person portrayed is a distant ancestor or a recently dead relative.[1]

Inscriptions and reliefs are in fact the most eloquent witnesses to this new form of heroization, not all of them as elaborate as the relief of Kydrogenes, but sometimes awkwardly written funerary inscriptions, verse and prose, and simple grave-monuments such as small altars. Because these private heroes seem so far below the glorious figures of classical

Greek myth and history, they tend to be taken as a sign of vulgarization and decadence. Thus the great Prussian Hellenist, Wilamowitz, wrote in his posthumous *Glaube der Hellenen:* "Later [after the classical period] there came about a broadening of the belief in heroes, in that it now only means that continuation after death is expected for the dead, and those left behind ascribe it to him on the gravestone. Every Tom, Dick and Harry is now elevated. Nobody thinks of a continued influence. It is as formulaic as 'the late *(der selige)* X.'" Similarly Arthur Darby Nock, speaking of the Roman imperial period: "While interest in the cult of the old heroes was intensified by the archaism which marked the Greek world in the first two centuries of our era, the application of the term *heros* to the recently dead was often a meaningless compliment."[2]

Above all, the great epigrapher and historian Louis Robert maintained that *hêrôs* or *hêrôis,* at least in inscriptions of the imperial period, meant simply that a person was dead. In his view, when one or these words was preceded by the term *neos,* which can mean either "young" or "new," the phrase meant no more than "who died young." Robert also observed that *hêrôs* sometimes appeared in the vocative phrase, *hêrôs chrêste,* "kindly hero," but did not explain how "kindly" was compatible with the notion that "hero" meant nothing more than "dead."[3]

It is certainly true that in the vast majority of cases, "hero" implies that a person is dead (though that is not the same as being lexically equivalent to "dead"), and that the examples of living heroes are very few. It can also be conceded that when the living commemorated their dead, especially those who had died young, they could have called them "young hero" or "kindly hero" without investing much belief in their words: so also a disgraced politician can say, "My mother was a saint," without implying that she has been formally canonized, and perhaps without having any belief in an afterlife at all. But because such language may sometimes have been formulaic and empty of meaning, it was not necessarily so always. In most cases there is no way of testing what the actual thoughts of those using such language were, any more than it is possible nowadays to infer the real feelings of those who speak of "saints" or "angels" when commemorating their loved ones. An examination of the ancient evidence shows that at least many of the bereaved who used such language invested it with real meaning.

Moreover, the simplicity of certain of these funerary monuments cannot be treated as an index of belief. A simple columnar monument found in the Athenian agora bears a two-word inscription, "Conon, hero *(Konôn hêrôs),*" which has elicited the modern observation, "The title means nothing more than 'the much respected and late lamented.'" As with modern tombstones, the degree of elaboration is not proportional to the intensity of belief, but instead reflects other factors, above all the economic conditions of the commemorator.[4]

This alleged "broadening" of heroization and devaluation of the term "hero" is in fact a societal change, whereby the wealthy upper classes of the Greek cities express their commemoration of their dead members in an increasingly public way; this fashion then travels downwards in society, so that even the modestly wealthy can club together to build *hêrôa* for themselves, or slaves can join in commemorating a valued fellow-slave. The beginning of this change can be seen about 200 B.C.E., and a major document of it is the will of Epicteta, a wealthy widow on the island of Thera (yet again, the Doric Thera stands out as a nursery of new heroes). Epicteta's husband, Phoenix, had begun to build a sanctuary of the Muses, a "Museum," in honor of their son Cratesilochos and in preparation for his own death and that of other members of the family. Unlike the shrine erected by Mnesiepes of Paros in honor of the Muses and Archilochos, the Museum of Epicteta was private and exclusive, and contained several *hêrôa* for individual members of the family. After Phoenix's death, their remaining son urged Epicteta to build one for himself, as for his father and his brother; he instructs his mother to found an association of her male relatives, and this group is to tend the Museum and the *hêrôa.* Over three days each year, the members are to lead a procession to the site, in which the women and children associated with the family will take part, and the participants are to sacrifice and to feast in honor of the Muses and the four heroes. The chief victim will be a sheep *(hierêion),* of which the meat is to be distributed in the customary way, though there is no mention of the blood being poured into the ground. In addition to their normal share, the goddesses receive a cake or loaf called an *ellutas,* but the heroes receive a different kind of cake *(parax)* and three fish *(opsaria)* as well, so that their food is similar to that eaten by their living relatives. This is a family-party, in which the dead join with the living, and as the rite has become more exclusive, it has also become less solemn and official.[5]

A long inscription from Aegiale on the island of Amorgos, dated to the late second century B.C.E., is a very expressive document of heroization, but unlike the will of Epicteta, it shows a convergence between public and private mourning that was to become more marked in the imperial period. A certain Aleximachos, the son of Critolaos, has died while still a youth, probably while still an "ephebe," that is, enrolled in the class of males aged roughly sixteen to eighteen who were trained by their cities in intellectual and physical pursuits. His father now establishes a foundation to commemorate him by giving the sum of two thousand drachmas, from the interest of which a public feast and an athletic contest *(agôn)* will be held. This foundation is a gift to the city, which first accepts it by decree *(psêphisma)* and then fixes the terms in a law *(nomos),* drawn up by a commission of three men appointed to "propose the heroization" *(graphein ton aphêrôismon).* The section of the law laying down the procedures to be followed has three parts. The first concerns the "public feast" *(dêmothoinia).* To ensure the proper conduct of this, the magistrates in office *(prytaneis)* are to select two supervisors *(epimelêtai)* not less than thirty years of age, who will purchase a bull not less than two years old. The president of the gymnasium *(gymnasiarchos)* and the ephebes, followed by "all the younger men," are to go in procession leading the bull, and then sacrifice it in a private house (presumably before the door or in the forecourt). Thereafter they will serve the meat at the feast and may, if they so decide, add extra money (the source is not specified) and invite a much larger number of people, including resident foreigners, visitors, and Romans. They will repeat all these arrangements a second day.

The next part of the law concerns the conduct of the contest. The supervisors will slaughter *(sphaxôsi)* a ram "of the finest quality" on the first day of the month by the cult-statue *(agalma)* that his father intends to set up to the dead Aleximachos; that is, these commemorative contests are to take place monthly and to begin with an *enagismos.* Before the statue they will set "a side-dish *(parathesis)* consisting of four half-*hekteis* of wheat [roughly equivalent to a day's grain ration for about fifteen men] and the roasted meat of the ram." On the next day they will hold the contest, with the prizes coming from the sale of half of the meat and wheat, while the other half is given to the magistrates and the supervisors. "They shall not have an entry for the *pancration* [a combination of boxing and wrestling], but Aleximachos son of Critolaos shall be announced as the victor." The last part of the law concerns sanctions aimed at safeguarding its provisions and ensuring its observation in perpetuity.[6]

The chief interest of the document is to show that, as probably in most cases, "heroization" signifies, not making someone a hero, but recognizing him as such by cultic acts. Just as the Amphipolitans passed a law *(nomos)* to sacrifice to Brasidas as hero, so here the law does not make the dead youth a hero: his heroic status is presumed, and what matters is to recognize it in perpetuity by a sacrifice before his statue followed by a public feast. His higher existence is especially evident in the contest. On the night before the contest, some of the food provided by the foundation is to be set before his statue, and those presiding over the contest will acknowledge his presence by crowning him as the ghostly victor in the pancration (he may have met his death in this most perilous and sanguinary of sports). While the city "heroizes" Aleximachos, it does so at the prompting and from the funds of his rich and influential father. There is thus a convergence between the purely private foundation of Epicteta and the older practice of communal heroization that goes back many centuries before.

This extravagance also begins to be reflected in funerary architecture of the later Hellenistic period and continues well into the imperial era. The building that Critolaos might have constructed for himself and his family (since the inscription only concerns his son's public commemoration) can be imagined from a *hêrôon* excavated at Calydon in northwestern Greece. The plan of this is almost rectangular, with a series of rooms on three sides and a peristyle court. This was supplied with a fountain and was used for certain athletics such as wrestling; on its west side was a curved space with a bench *(exedra),* and in the middle of the north side was a cult-room, from which a flight of steps led to an underground crypt. This in turn contained two stone couches, equipped with footstools and pillows, on which the bodies of the dead were probably placed. In the cult-room above was found a statue-base with a fragmentary inscription showing that a certain Pantaleon dedicated a statue of his wife to "the hero Leon, the new Heracles," who is probably the ancestor of the family. The building also contained many sculptural fragments representing gods such as Zeus, Aphrodite, and Heracles, and young men who may be heroized family-members. This is therefore a huge private tomb, almost resembling a gymnasium in size and form. At the same time, its location in a necropolis south of the city shows that it was not for general use, but for the family and its close associates, like Epicteta's Museum.[7]

In due course, the extravagant structures of the Hellenistic east began to be imitated in republican Rome, before becoming usual among the wealthy of the Roman Empire. Cicero's planned shrine *(fanum)* for his dead daughter Tullia was intended for her "apotheosis," a term compatible with her being a heroine rather than a goddess.[8] About a century later, a certain Epicrates from Nacrasos in the province of Asia provides for the commemoration of his dead son, much as Critolaos had done on Amorgos centuries before. As the head of a mixed Greek and Roman household, Epicrates sets aside a parcel of land to be the monument *(mnêmeion)* of the "hero Daiphantos." His motive is "not only my affectionate feeling towards my child, but the fact that the hero often visited me in dreams, signs and visions." The two freedmen charged with the maintenance of the tomb, which is also intended to contain Epicrates himself and other family-members, "will adorn the tomb with roses *(rhodisousin)*, spending no less than twenty-five drachmas on roses, doing this expressly for worship *(thrêskeia)* of the hero." Epicrates imposes a fearful curse on possible violators. "If any does something contrary to these (dispositions), he shall be guilty of tomb-robbing; even so let him find the gods in heaven and below the earth and the heroes as well angry and implacable." A series of imprecations follows, ending with the cryptic phrase, "and other curses are stored up for those who contravene this my will." There is no sign that the belief in the reality or the power of heroes was in any way weaker in this mixed Graeco-Roman family of western Asia Minor than in Hellenistic or even classical Greece.[9]

Like the surviving documents and building-complexes, Greek grave-reliefs from the third century onwards show motifs that imply the continued existence of the dead, and either implicitly or by means of an accompanying inscription mark them as a hero or (much less frequently) a heroine. A frequent motif is the so-called funerary-meal, or more

Pl. 3. Heroic relief, Pergamon (courtesy of the Deutsches Archäologisches Institut, Istanbul; photo by W. Schiele, 1980; negative number Perg. 67-3.2)

accurately "meal for the dead" *(Totenmahl),* similar to that laid down by Epicteta in her will, though because of the exigencies of space only a few participants are shown. Usually a single male reclines as for a banquet, with a table beside him holding simple foods such as cakes and fruit. Often a woman sits at his feet, and with her are children, servants, household items, and pets. Sometimes a horse stands in the background with his head outlined by what looks like a small window, and large snakes may be shown coiled around the branches of a tree, or actually reaching for the food on the table (Pl. 3).[10]

At least in part, these banquet scenes are "memory-pictures," recalling meals taken in life, but now transformed so that the dead dines either

Pl. 4. Relief showing Polydeucion, Brauron, Attica (courtesy of the 2nd Ephorate of
Prehistoric and Historic Antiquities, Greece)

alone or in the company of those left behind. According to Lucian, the
wealthy sophist Herodes Atticus mourned his favorite Polydeuces, also
known more familiarly as "Polydeucion," by having a coach made ready
for the boy to drive and a meal laid for him. A funerary relief that
Herodes set up at the sanctuary of Brauron in Attica shows Polydeuces
reclining at a banquet while a horse's head is visible in the background.
At the sophist's estate of Cephissia, where his favorite was buried, he or-
ganized commemorative contests in his memory; an extant inscription
shows a group of officials appointed to keep order, "baton-carriers"
(rhabdophoroi), honoring "the hero Polydeuces" (Pl. 4).[11]

That such banquet-reliefs are memory-pictures is further implied by
their resemblance to domestic dinners. It was customary in Greece, and in
Rome also down to the imperial period, for men to recline at dinner while
women and children sat apart, usually on chairs; the only exceptions were
prostitutes, euphemistically called "companions" or "hired women" *(het-
airae, meretrices)*, and established mistresses or "friends" *(philai, amicae)*.[12]

Reliefs, and also painted tombstones, show exactly this arrangement, even when the person commemorated is a woman. A series of monuments from Lilybaion in western Sicily, the modern Marsala, is dated on stylistic grounds to the first century C.E. They consist of limestone *naïskoi* (miniature temples), with painted scenes of the deceased. Every one of the series shows a man and a woman feasting in the afterlife, though the inscription names only a single person. One such monument commemorates a woman with the Semitic name of Maria as a "good heroine" *(hêrus agatha)*. She is seated on a chair, while an unnamed male, presumably her husband, reclines on a couch. In the foreground is a three-legged table on which stands food, apparently three loaves or cakes. The man holds out a goblet to the woman, while above them are objects which, though not certainly identifiable, must refer to her occupations in life: a tambourine *(tympanon)*, a pair of ribbonlike objects (perhaps headbands), a pair of castanets *(krotaloi)*, a fan, a basket, and what may be another pair of castanets (Pl. 5).[13]

The domestic nature of these scenes also appears in the depiction of children, servants, and dogs, though the animal most frequently represented is the snake. As has been seen, the Hesiodic *Catalogue of Women* introduced a snake into its account of the preliminaries to the Trojan War, and snakes also appear on the "hero-reliefs" of archaic Sparta. A Spartan king is the subject of one of the best-known stories about heroes and snakes. The biographer Plutarch tells how the Spartan king Cleomenes had gone to Egypt to serve Ptolemy Euergetes, but fell into disfavor with Euergetes' corrupt successor, Ptolemy Philopator, and was killed in a skirmish. When Philopator ordered Cleomenes' dead body to be crucified, "those who were guarding [it] where it hung saw a huge snake coiled about the head and protecting the face, so that no carnivorous bird could attack it . . . The Alexandrians actually venerated him, coming to the place and calling Cleomenes a hero and the offspring of gods." As a Platonist, Plutarch mistrusts any suggestion that the dead can enter a higher state of being immediately and without intervening purification. Hence, he prefers the scientific explanation given by the "wiser" Alexandrians that the juices of rotting bodies produce snakes, "and because they observed this, the ancients associated the snake with heroes more than any other animal."[14]

Pl. 5. Monument of "heroine" Maria, Lilybaion, Sicily (by permission of the Assessorato dei Beni Culturali e Ambientali e della Pubblica Istruzione, Soprintendenza per i Beni Culturali ed Ambiental—Servizio per i Beni Archeologici—TRAPANI)

Thus the association is clear, but not the reasons for it, which may have differed between times, places, and even persons. One reason is presumably the idea of protection, as when the snake protects the body of Cleomenes. For Theophrastus in the late fourth century, if the super-stitious man sees a snake of the type called *hieros* ("holy"), he will im-mediately set up a *hêrôon*. Here the association may be a double one, that the snake suggests the presence of a hero, but also that the hero can both use the creature to punish and at the same time give protection against it, since the "holy" snake was especially venomous. A verse in-scription of the late Hellenistic period commemorates an aged warrior, Apollonios, who used the image of a snake as a talisman on his tomb as he had on his shield in his lifetime:

> Now having died an old man, upon himself he placed this serpent
> To be a fierce guardian of the doors of this tomb;
> He had it also upon his shield when he toiled in the works of Ares,
> Devising many sorrows against his enemies.[15]

The snakes shown in hero-reliefs are sometimes seen as "chthonic" or sinister, an association explained by their living in the earth or casting their skin, but the reliefs only show them coiled in the branches of trees, or less often around tables or altars. The snake that is now called the *col-uber Aesculapii,* and is probably the house-snake of the ancients, closely fits the representation on these hero-reliefs: "It grows to the length of five feet, climbs extremely well, feeds chiefly on mice, and becomes very tame."[16] Thus the representations of snakes on so many funerary reliefs can have many meanings, but in the Hellenistic and Roman periods three predominate: the snake as memory-picture of life on earth, as em-blem or symbol of existence after death, and as guardian of the tomb and the space around it.

The other animal that constantly appears in such reliefs is the horse, shown mainly in two ways. He may appear with his head protruding from a small aperture or window, perhaps meant to suggest a stable door, as in the relief of Kydrogenes. The horse shown in the relief for Poly-deuces at Brauron is a late, archaizing version of this scheme. At other times the dead, sometimes a woman, is shown riding horseback.[17]

Here again interpretations differ, as they must also have differed for the ancient viewer. Like the snake, the horse when not shown in a domestic context was associated with life after death, sometimes with life as a hero, as when coins of Hadrian's favorite Antinoos associate the late hero with the image of a horse. The horse is also associated with strength and protection. Reliefs from Thrace frequently show a hero on horseback whose name differs from region to region: thus at Odessos on the Pontic coast, he is "the Hero Karabasmos" and is shown riding towards an altar, behind which a tiny human figure stands carrying a plate full of offerings on his head, while before the altar a bull waits to be sacrificed. In Anatolia a divinity called the "Saving One" *(Sôzôn)*, sometimes associated with Zeus or Apollo, is usually shown on horseback, and similarly the indigenous god Kakasbos rides a horse and carries a massive club. When shown together with scenes of family life, the horse perhaps suggested wealth, of which it was a characteristic symbol. The deceased when shown on horseback may be a protector of the living, or may appear as he was imagined in the next life.[18]

In these reliefs, "hero" is not a "meaningless compliment," but suggests an existence or influence in the afterlife, and the texts that accompany them tell the same tale. Many are simple prose salutations addressed to the dead, of the form: "Sopater son of Stratonides, hero, hail" *(Sôpatros Stratônidou hêrôs chaire)*, with the hero shown as a long-haired boy, accompanied by an attendant and a faithful dog. Women heroines are particularly common on Samos: one relief says, "Lais, wife of Phoenix, heroine, hail" *(Lais Phoinikos hêroinê, chaire)*, and the wife sits while her husband reclines in the standard banqueting pose. The dead person can also be addressed as "kindly hero" *(hêrôs chrêste)*. Other epithets, only used of males in these reliefs, are "young *or* new hero" *(neos hêrôs)* and "manifest hero" *(hêrôs epiphanês)*, both salutations accompanying figures on horseback. A Roman legionary is shown standing in full armor as "a soldier of the eleventh cohort, beneficent hero" *(hêrôs agathopoios)*, while below him appears military equipment with the addition of a harp *(cithara)*, perhaps meant to suggest war-booty (Pl. 6).[19]

Certainly the epigrams that accompany some of these reliefs use much of the pessimistic language habitual in Greek funerary poetry: Fate *(Moira)*, Malice *(Phthonos)*, Destiny *(daimôn)*. Yet very many also

Pl. 6. A Roman soldier commemorated as a hero, Selymbria

express a hope or expectation that the dead, whether or not he or she is a hero, can communicate with the living or enjoy a blessed existence in the afterlife. A late Hellenistic gravestone from near Smyrna shows a young man called Dionysios who had died at age seventeen, "leaving harsh grief to his parents, but attaining to heavenly birth; for leaving the mortal part of life, he is equal to the immortal heroes, having the same sanctuary *(temenos)* as they." Probably Dionysios' parents had built a shrine for him in which divinities such as Heracles also received cult, like the *hêrôon* at Calydon in Aetolia. At Ephesus, a woman who has placed two sons in a single "mournful tomb" prays to Hermes:

"Maia's son, guard my sons among the heroes, you who always travel to the place of the Pious"; the relief shows one of the two brothers sitting, while the other stands with a horse's head just visible in the background. On Samos, bereaved parents supplicate the judge of the underworld for their dead son: "Minos, who supremely passes judgment over mortals, enshrine the youth in the place of the Pious." At Miletoupolis in Mysia, Asclepiades, the son of a doctor, "after loosing the cables of swift-fated fortune" and "leaving griefs to my mother and brother," ends by saying, "But they weep, while I sit among the sons of the immortals, a pupil of the son of Phoebus." Though he continues his studies in the next world under Asclepius, the relief shows him banqueting while his mother sits before him in an attitude of mourning.[20]

An especially expressive epigram of this kind, though it concerns a heroization that is both private and public like that of Aleximachos of Aegiale, honors a certain Leonteus, also from Aegiale. Above it is written in prose, "The people to Leonteus son of Eurydicos, hero": "hero" gains especial prominence as the only word in its line. The epigram says: "Leonteus son of Eurydicos here, who shone with virtue, his fatherland honored in the precinct of the gymnasium. For he had just left the *chlamys* [the cloak worn by ephebes] when, a new source of grief, he went to Hades aged eighteen, leaving tears to his mother. His city honored him with crowns and this tomb, indicating the virtue of his noble ancestors too. Ah, spindles of the Fates, tireless, compelling; may you send this (man) to the holy home of the Pious." Here too the youth is imagined as going to Hades and at the same time to the islands of the Pious.[21]

Heroes and heroines were not always imagined as living in the underworld or the Blessed Isles, but could also dwell in heaven close to the gods. The semiliterate epigram of a young woman called Stratonice at Ephesos, who is shown sitting before an altar with a dog gazing at her, reads: "This tomb holds the lovely body of one who died prematurely, for when she was sixteen years old Koure the wife of Plouteus took you to Hades. But the blessed gods, pitying her, did not leave her soul to enter within the house of Hades: she has flown in air to heaven, and among the gods Stratonice has a fate equal to a heroine. If anyone had seen her whom the tomb holds when she lived, he would not have passed this place without a tear."[22]

A heroine of the imperial period is the subject of the longest and most elaborate of such commemorative poems. Regilla, the wife of the great second-century sophist, Herodes Atticus, was buried on their joint estate near Rome, and Herodes commissioned a fashionable poet of the day, Marcellus of Side, to commemorate her. The text describes her as "dwelling with the heroines in the Blessed Isles, where Cronos holds sway." Friends or passersby are invited to "bring holy gifts and to sacrifice: there is no need of sacrifices given unwillingly, but it is good for the pious to show concern with heroes too. For she is not mortal, and yet not a goddess: hence she has received neither a holy temple nor a tomb, nor gifts like those fit for mortals nor those fit for gods." Excessive as these sentiments may appear, they are basically no different from the funerary epigrams of the less wealthy, which also represent the dead as dwelling in the Blessed Isles or consorting with the heroes in the hereafter.[23]

All such effusions might seem to belong to a world remote from actual belief, like the invocation of the Muses in eighteenth-century English poetry. It is less possible to argue away the language of a prose writer contemporary with Herodes, Aelius Aristides. Aristides had close connections with Cyzicus, and one of his works is a lament for a Cyzicene pupil called Eteoneus who had died on the verge of manhood. On both sides he had belonged to the flower of the city's aristocracy, though only his mother and brothers were still living. Comparing the dead youth to a hero, Aristides imagines some god appearing like a *deus ex machina* in tragedy and comforting the citizens in these words: "Cease, mortals. The lad, or rather man, is not to be mourned or to be pitied for the journey he has now traveled, but more than anyone he is fortunate in relation to human affairs. Neither Cocytos nor Acheron has carried him away, nor will some urn take and hide him. For the rest of time hereafter he will roam celebrated and ageless as a hero, seated beside Cyzicus, honored by ancestral Apollo as were Amyclas, Narcissos, Hyakinthos, and anyone else who besides a beautiful form possessed a higher virtue *(aretê)* than the human kind . . . If anyone thinks that he did not have sufficient enjoyment of glory, you should now complete it by the additional honor of a hero, for all his praises are at last assured." Similarly the author known as Menander Rhetor, writing a handbook of public speaking about a century after Aristides, urges that the speech of consolation should contain exhortations such as: "I feel convinced that he who has gone dwells in the Elysian Fields, where dwell Rhadamanthus and Menelaus . . . Or rather perhaps he is living now with the gods, traveling round the sky and looking down on this world." So also in the funeral speech: "No need to lament: he is sharing the community of gods *(politeuetai meta tôn theôn)*, or dwells in the Elysian Fields." Certainly Aristides and Menander are drawing on the language of literature, and death often leads the living to seek consolation in beliefs that do not form part of their usual lives. But like a preacher in a modern funeral service, public speakers must have sought words that would resonate with their listeners' beliefs or hopes about the next world.[24]

In the imperial period, the term *hêrôon,* so often used in earlier centuries for the tomb of a mythical hero or a fallen warrior such as Brasidas, sometimes indicates an ordinary tomb. Persons erect *hêrôa* for themselves and their families; quite often there is no physical difference between a *hêrôon* and a monument called by a different name, of which there was a large variety in the Greek world.[25] But for some *hêrôa* a form of cult is certain. An Athenian inscription of imperial date contains the rules for a club *(eranos)* to which the members contribute to ensure their own burial in the *hêrôon.* They call their group "the most solemn association of club-members" *(hê semnotatê synodos tôn eranistôn)* and no one may join unless he is pure, pious, and good *(hagnos kai eusebês kai agathos).* They are to have a full range of officials, including a scribe and an "adjunct priest," designated by the almost unexampled term *homoleitôr,* who is to be put in charge of the *hêrôon* for life. Any member who causes disturbances or fights will be ejected, and in addition will be liable either to a monetary fine or to a whipping. This curious but not unparalleled document shows that this *hêrôon* is far from an ordinary tomb. Those having the right of burial have to be in a state of ritual purity; they have club-dinners, presumably within the precincts of the tomb, but any rowdy behavior on such occasions brings not only expulsion but punishment.[26]

Individuals make similar provisions. At Ephesos, a wealthy citizen called Peplos draws up an agreement with the city for the upkeep of his family *hêrôon.* It already contains the body of his wife, and a remarkable inventory of the contents details "the implements for the performance of the heroic cult" *(ta skeue eis tên hupêresian tou hêrôismou)*: a large number of statues of the dead woman, as well as a "tripod" (a small dining-table of the kind often shown in funerary reliefs), and at least seven chairs or benches. Peplos also institutes a college of "hero-worshipers" *(hêrôstai)*, making careful provision to ensure that their number will remain constant. The ruins of Termessos in Pisidia have preserved a series of sumptuous *hêrôa* of the second and third centuries that exemplify the kind of building envisaged by Peplos. The grandest, built by a wealthy widow for her late husband, her two sons, and herself, contains a "house" *(oikos)* with two sarcophagi, one for the married couple, one for the sons, and in addition portrait-statues of the deceased *(andriantes)*; this "house" is entered by a high door, fronted by four columns, and before it stands an altar. The whole complex is fenced off by a wall *(peribolos)* and an inscription over the entrance of the "house" declares that no one is to bury any remains inside the complex other than those of the widow. At a lower social level, a group of eight slaves at Patara in Lycia dedicates an altar in memory of their fellow-slave, Calocairos, a "good man, hero" *(anêr agathos, hêrôs)* and "devoted to his master" *(philokurios)*. The group presumably used the altar when they sacrificed and dined in memory of their colleague, a humbler version of the funerary association established by the wealthy Peplos at Ephesos.[27]

Curiously, Christians sometimes call their tombs *hêrôa*. Thus at Apamea in Phrygia in the third century, a certain Aurelius Trophimos builds a *hêrôon* "for myself and my wife Aur(elia) Antoniana, into which no-one else shall be put; and if any one tries, he will answer for it to God." Below is carved the word *icthys* ("fish"), and this, as well as the formula "he will answer for it to God," marks the couple as Christians. An inscription of the same city, dated as late as 600, designates a *hêrôon* reserved for "the most excellent intoners of psalms, orthodox."[28] This might suggest that for Christians the word *hêrôon* had lost all association with pagan beliefs about the afterlife. Yet Christians took no offense at the word "hero." We shall see that their apologists distinguished heroes from the gods who were reputed to have engendered them; that was a fiction invented by demons, who wanted to destroy the uniqueness of the only Son of God. Unlike the gods, who were demons in disguise, the heroes could provide models for right conduct; Augustine held that Christian martyrs would have a much better right to be called by the name than the heroes of paganism "if the ecclesiastical mode of speaking allowed it."[29]

For some pagans the word "hero" may have lost its ancient force, though whether this represents degeneration rather than evolution is a matter of debate. But it is beyond question that for many, and not just for those of the educated classes, the word "hero" continued to convey the idea of a continued existence and power after death. Epicrates' son could appear to him in dreams, urging him to set up a family "memorial"; a funerary association can insist on the ritual purity of its members and establish a priest to look after its property; writers in prose and verse can describe the late hero dwelling in the Blessed Isles or with the gods in heaven. The view that the word "hero" means no more than the French "défunt," German "der Selige," Arthur Darby Nock's "meaningless compliment," is also inconsistent with the exaltation of public heroes in the imperial period, since the same word can hardly be meaningless when applied to one set of heroes and meaningful when applied to others. These public heroes are the last and, in the person of Antinoos, the most conspicuous example of heroization in the ancient world.

CHAPTER 6

Greek Heroes in a Roman World

✦

The Roman Empire in the period of its greatest stability and prosperity, from the beginning of the Flavian dynasty to the end of the Severan, saw an unprecedented convergence between the interests of the rulers and the upper class of the Greek cities. If there were still undercurrents of nostalgia or resentment, in general the Greek literature of the time, most of it produced by members of this upper class, presents a smooth and polished surface of acceptance of the present combined with celebration of a glorious past. In this era, which towards its close was not without intimations of trouble to come, an antiquarian vogue among the Greek aristocracy both called the old heroes to new life, and added to the roll of new heroes by public commemoration, often of young males snatched away by premature death.

The biographer and Platonic philosopher Plutarch exemplifies this combination of reverence for the past and engagement with the present. He begins his paired biographies of *Theseus and Romulus,* the earliest in time of his subjects, with a declaration about the boundary between myth and history. Geographers cram what is beyond their knowledge on the very edges of their maps, dismissing it as "waterless desert," "trackless marsh," or "frozen sea." Though the two founders of Athens and Rome might seem equally remote, Plutarch has nevertheless decided to include them, trusting that he can "purge the mythical by the use of reason, and give it the appearance of history." There was no lack of previous writers who had written accounts of Theseus and other heroes, but Plutarch's innovation was to push the boundaries of history backwards so as to include the legendary founders of Athens and Rome, the twin poles of power and culture, in a series that came down to a few generations before his own. Like other Greeks, Plutarch did not regard great men who were almost legendary as existing outside of historical time.[1]

Plutarch strongly disapproved of those Hellenistic kings who declared themselves gods, and he may well have had unexpressed reservations about the official deification of Roman emperors, but heroes were another matter. In discussing the apotheosis of Romulus, he observes: "We must not commit the unnatural act of sending the bodies of good men to heaven together (with their souls). But we may certainly believe, in accordance with nature and divine justice, that their souls are carried up from men to heroes, from heroes to spirits *(daimones);* and from spirits, if they are completely purified as in a mystery-rite *(teletê)*, they arrive in truth and in accordance with probability among the gods."[2]

In the number of such heroes Plutarch must have placed certain ancestors of his own and of his friends. One of his sons was named "Chaeron" after the founder of Chaeronea. Though so-called herophoric names are frequent in this period, it is likely that as a local aristocrat Plutarch's family claimed descent from the founding hero of the city. Addressing his brother in one of his dialogs, he says, "You and your family . . . feel entitled to greater consideration than others in Boeotia as descendants of Opheltas, and again in Phocis from your connection with Daiphantos; you moreover lent me your presence and support the other day when I helped the Lycormai and Satilaioi to recover the hereditary honor of the descendants of Heracles, the right to wear a crown. I said at the time that the posterity of Heracles should particularly be maintained in possession of the honors and rewards he had earned by his services to the Greeks for which he had received no adequate thanks or compensation himself." Of the persons mentioned here, Opheltas is a legendary king from Thessaly, some of whose followers settled in Chaeronea, and Daiphantos of Hyampolis was a warrior of the early fifth century who still received "honors and sacrifices" from his citizens in the author's own day; the Lycormai and Satilaioi are unknown, but must be some Boeotian family claiming descent from Heracles. The passage perfectly expresses the aristocratic claims of Plutarch and the class to which he belonged, and the same pride must lie behind the biographies, now lost, that he wrote of Heracles and Daiphantos. So also his lost biography of the

Messenian hero Aristomenes was an expression of local pride, since the Boeotian Epaminondas (yet another subject of a Plutarchan biography) was regarded as the second liberator and founder of Messene, as the shadowy Aristomenes was the first.[3]

Other of Plutarch's friends belonged to a similar level of society elsewhere in Greece. Themistocles, once his fellow-student at Athens, descended from the great Athenian politician and general, who had passed his last years comfortably installed by the Persian king in Magnesia on the Maeander. There he was honored as a founder and had a sumptuous tomb in the agora that was still standing Plutarch's time, while the family continued to receive honors from the Magnesians, as Plutarch's own ancestor Daiphantos was honored in Hyampolis. Another of the biographer's friends descended from the Achaean statesman Aratus, who was heroized by the Sicyonians, though by the author's time his cult had fallen into neglect.[4]

Claims of descent from such heroes, especially those of "heroic times," took on a new urgency in the reign of Hadrian, an emperor with a conspicuous devotion to the Greek past. When the action of the sea uncovered the tomb of Ajax in the Troad, the emperor kissed the exposed bones before building a new tomb over them; on passing through the obscure village of Melissa in northern Phrygia, where Alcibiades had died, he had a statue in Parian marble placed on the tomb and gave orders that a bull should be sacrificed there every year. When he established the Panhellenion or league of "all Greeks," most of the cities that obtained admittance did so by proving that heroes were their founders, a process in which the claim that their leading families were of heroic descent must have had special weight.[5]

In the Hellenistic period, cities heroized their sons for acting as "saviors" and "founders" either in battle or by diplomacy, and wealthy persons such as Epicteta of Thera honored their family's dead, though usually without claiming for them any exceptional merit. In the imperial period, while families continued to heroize their own members, Greek cities now did the same for their own nobility, not only when induced to do so by a wealthy individual like Critolaos of Amorgos, but of their own accord, especially when a young man's death could mean the extinction of a line of public benefactors. Titus Statilius Lamprias of

Epidauros died at the age of seventeen, probably about the middle of the first century of our era. By descent he was related to the ancient family of the *Kêrykes (Heralds)* in Athens, which had a traditional role in the celebration of the Eleusinian Mysteries. At Argos his ancestors included Perseus, the son of Zeus and Danae, while at Sparta they included Heracles and the general Lysander. Lysander was not only the great general who led Sparta and its allies to victory in the Peloponnesian War, he was also the first Greek to receive public honors as a god in his own lifetime. The decrees of Athens and of Sparta qualify Lamprias as a "hero" and take the form of a "decree of consolation," a type known mainly from the imperial period, some of which also qualify their subjects as a "hero" or "heroine."[6]

A "hero" similar to Lamprias in the first century is Tiberius Claudius Paulinus in second-century Pergamum. He too comes from a noble family of the city; his father was a generous and active citizen, "useful to the city in every respect," and his son acted as "hymnode" (singer in a chorus of young males) for the emperor Hadrian. On his death, which may well have occurred in his youth or early middle age, his fellow citizens interred him in a *hêrôon*. The altar is inscribed: "To the gods below and to Tiberius Claudius Paulinus, hero, the altar and the surrounding structure *(perioikodomêma)* have been consecrated as holy and inaccessible to all humans." As in the inscription for Lamprias, the word "hero" stands alone and centered in the fourth line, in a way that is inconceivable if it meant only "the late" (Pl. 7). The whole tenor of the text shows that the *hêrôon* was sacred and inviolable, and that the altar served for sacrifice to the "hero" and to the gods of the dead.[7] At Mallos in Cilicia a cylindrical statue-base is inscribed, "The people of Mallos (erected) the *hêrôon* to Flavia Procla, heroine *(hêrôis)*" (the last word again centered), and the life-size statue must have stood in a similar sanctuary.[8]

Paulinus is not the only civic hero of Pergamum. Another inscription records an inquiry made by the city to Apollo's oracle at Didyma, asking where to bury the "heroes" Marcellus and Rufinus "because of their past virtuousness of life." The first of these two men is unknown, but the second is one of Pergamum's most prominent benefactors, the donor of the great temple of Zeus Asclepios, Lucius Cuspius Rufinus. As the divine father of Asclepius, Apollo would naturally take an interest in the question,

Pl. 7. The inscription of Claudius Paulinus, Pergamon (courtesy of the Deutsches Archäologisches Institut, Istanbul; photo by E. Steiner, 1967; negative number R17.504)

and though his reply is not preserved, it presumably ordained some place within the limits of the city, a privilege usually preserved for exceptional personages. Here again the word "hero" must mean more than merely "deceased."[9]

Sometimes having heroic blood in the family in its turn encouraged heroization in the present. Philostratus describes a sophist called Marcus of Byzantium who was descended from Byzas, a son of Poseidon and the eponymous founder of the city; in one version of his myth, he brought the first settlers from Megara. Coins of Byzantium show Marcus with his Roman family-name, "Memmius," and certain of these carry an image of Byzas. Thanks to his heroic ancestry, he was able to reconcile Megara and Athens when the two cities were engaged in one of those quarrels between neighbors so frequent in the imperial period. Philostratus reports that Marcus stood out among the well-groomed tribe of second-century sophists for his unkempt hair and beard, and these features may also be part of his heroic image, since tangled hair is a regular trait of representations of Poseidon in this period.[10] The coins show Marcus as the "sacred recorder" *(hieromnêmôn),* the annual magistrate of Byzantium whose tenure gave its name to the year, and hence is called "eponymous." It was a customary practice of the age for individuals or families to set up a foundation to help defray the expenses of such offices, so that a deceased person could hold it posthumously as a hero or heroine, while a living substitute performed whatever work the office entailed. Marcus served as "sacred recorder" both in his lifetime and as a hero, and given his claims of descent from Poseidon and Byzas, the word "hero" must again mean more than simply "the late."[11]

An inscription from Naples contains documents of a *phratria* (religious brotherhood) named after the goddess Artemis, the "Artemisioi." The benefactor, a certain Munatius Hilarianus, is thanked by the association for his many gifts to it, which include a dining-room *(hestiatorion)* and a temple of the goddess. In return the members offer him four portrait-statues *(andriantes)* of himself and his late son, "Marius Verus the hero," but by a traditional gesture of modesty he accepts only a single painting *(graphê)* and a single statue of himself and "my son, your hero." As so often, it is the deceased male scion of a prominent family who is honored, but the expression "your hero," which has no parallel elsewhere, implies something more. Cities of this period, or some body within them such as the council *(boulê),* sometimes bestow such titles as "mother of the city," "son of the council," on prominent members of local society, and in the present text, the brotherhood votes to consider *(nomizein)* Hilarianus as its "champion" *(prostatês)* and "father" *(patêr).* The best explanation of the expression "your hero" is that the brothers had earlier voted to adopt the late Verus as their "hero" and probably to commemorate his birthday with feasting, prayers, and toasts.[12]

Though new heroes created by families or communities disappeared after the middle of the third century, there remained those created at the beginning of classical antiquity by the Homeric poems. The era of the Roman Empire at its most prosperous and stable, from the first century to the third, saw a movement in Greek literature that its first chronicler, Philostratus of Athens, called the "Second Sophistic," seeing the great public speakers of his age as descendants of the sophists of the classical period. Sophists such as Dio Chrysostom and Philostratus himself produced alternative versions of the Trojan War, arguing that it had not taken place at all, or at least had followed a different course from that narrated by Homer.[13]

The only work surviving from antiquity explicitly devoted to the subject of heroes is Philostratus' *Heroikos* or *Heroic Discourse,* which belongs approximately to the 220s. The setting is a lonely spot near the city of Elaious in the Thracian Chersonese, facing the Troad across the Dardanelles, and the two speakers are a Phoenician merchant, who is on a voyage towards the Euxine (the Black Sea), and a local vine-grower whose property is near the tomb of the hero Protesilaos. He was the first of the heroes to die at Troy, killed just as he jumped from his ship onto Trojan soil, and the Homeric Catalogue of Ships gives him a tantalizingly brief mention: before his early death at Troy, he left behind him a wife who tore both her cheeks in grief, and a house only half-finished. Philostratus describes his statue in the sanctuary, showing the hero on the prow of his ship, and speaks of the tomb as a low hill *(kolônos).* Coins of Elaious show the statue, and the hill can be identified with a prehistoric mound or *tell* standing some five hundred meters from the present shoreline. It is thus one of several such mounds that later Greeks took to be the burial place of a hero (Pl. 8).[14]

The essential premise of the work is that the vine-grower is in personal contact with Protesilaos, who returns in bodily form to the land around his tomb, just as in myth he returned after death to his wife Laodameia. In the preliminary part of the dialog, the vine-grower must first overcome the skepticism of the merchant. After doing that, he proceeds to report Protesilaos' description of the principal heroes of Troy, and incidentally to correct and amplify the account of Homer, so that the work belongs in the tradition that includes Dares, Dictys, and Dio Chrysos-

Pl. 8. Coin showing hero Protesilaos, Elaious (courtesy of the Staatliche Münzsammlung, Munich)

tom. The gallery of heroes culminates with Achilles and describes how he resides with Helen on an island in the Euxine. Excavations on this island, lying some fifty kilometers off the Danube delta, have revealed traces of his cult well into the third century.[15]

Achilles is again a powerful presence in what may be the last of the Greek romances, the *Aethiopica* or *Ethiopian Tale* of Heliodorus, whom some have thought a contemporary of Philostratus and others have dated to the later fourth century. Theagenes, the male protagonist (the "hero" in the modern, literary sense), is a descendant of Achilles from Hypata in Thessaly and enters the story as the head of a sacred delegation *(theôria)* sent to Delphi with the mission of sacrificing to Achilles' son, Neoptolemos. Theagenes is described in detail, with blond hair, flaring nostrils, and dark blue eyes, and as "truly worthy of the line of Achilles." He falls in love with Chariclea, the adoptive daughter of the priest of Apollo whose parents are later revealed as the king and queen of Ethiopia. The lovers are united in the last book, after Theagenes has undergone the ordeal of wrestling a bull to the ground, a form of bullfight for which the Thessalians were famous. Thus the descendant of Achilles marries the princess of a land that is already distant and fabulous in the *Iliad* and the *Odyssey*.[16] Whatever the correct date of Heliodorus, third century or fourth, it announces the Late Antique reverence for the heroes of classical myth, above all those of Homer.

CHAPTER 7

Antinoos

The imperial age perpetuates the practice of personal heroization already known from the late Hellenistic period, but combines it with a more intense cultivation of the traditional heroes, encouraged in this direction above all by the philhellenic emperor Hadrian. The most far-reaching of all heroizations of antiquity is that of Hadrian's own favorite Antinoos who drowned in the Nile, by accident or suicide, in the year 130. Some ancient observers, especially Christian ones, regarded the cult of Antinoos as the enshrinement of pederasty, while modern observers, more tolerant of same-sex attachments, have tended to emphasize its erotic or romantic aspects, sometimes to the neglect of its place in the history of Greek religion.[1]

The manner and the consequences of Antinoos' death are obscure in their details, but the outlines are clear. He was born in Bithynion, later called Claudiopolis, a minor city lying in a rich agricultural region of eastern Bithynia; the date of his birth, the circumstance of his first meeting with Hadrian, and indeed the precise nature of their relationship, are uncertain, but he could have been as much as thirty at the time of his death. He was not city-born, but rather from the surrounding territory or *chôra* of Bithynion, and hence the frequent assimilation of him after his death with divinities of the outdoors such as Artemis, Dionysus, and Silvanus; he himself is honored in some places as a god, in others as a hero. In his memory Hadrian founded Antinooupolis, "Antinoos' City," at the place on the Nile where his favorite had drowned.[2]

In considering the cult of Antinoos, it is essential to distinguish the parts taken by Hadrian, by the cities of Egypt, and by cities of the other provinces and of Italy. At his Tiburtine villa, Hadrian set up at least one statue of Antinoos in the form of Osiris, which is now in the Vatican. If the recent excavators are correct in their inferences, he buried the youth's body, perhaps mummified, in a sumptuous monument now dubbed the *Antinoeion,* though as yet there is no ancient authority for the name. The excavators have also found what may well be the base of the "obelisk of Antinoos" that now stands on the Pincio in Rome (Pl. 9). The text of this, in hieroglyphics, says that he is buried in the gardens of the emperor and is a now a god called Osiris-Antinoos, who hears the prayers of his worshipers and heals their diseases; contests are held in his honor and sacrifices made to him at Antinooupolis. According to Cassius Dio, Hadrian dedicated "portrait-statues *(andriantes),* or rather cult-statues *(agalmata)*" for Antinoos "across almost the whole world," and welcomed flatterers who said that a star had been born from his soul. Poets and orators consoled the emperor by averring that the late Antinoos now resided on the moon, or that a new flower had sprung up from the blood of a lion that he and Hadrian had killed together. All this is consistent with Hadrian's regarding him either as a hero, as Alexander had treated Hephaestion, or as a god; the text of the obelisk refers only to Antinoos' cult in Egypt, where there is no doubt of his divinity.[3]

Hadrian's new foundation of Antinooupolis was to be a Greek settlement, with a constitution drawn up by the emperor and with special privileges; at the same time, it stood at the head of a major route across the mountains to the Red Sea and had a commercial as well as a commemorative importance. The tribes into which the citizens were divided all took their names from the imperial family except only "Oseirantinoos." The anti-Christian Platonist Celsus, writing about a generation after the foundation, compared the honors paid by the new city to Antinoos with those paid by Christians to Jesus, and also compared the notoriously immoral sect of the Carpocratians with "revelers" *(thiasôtai)* of Antinoos in Egypt. As a Platonist, Celsus, like Plutarch before him, would have found such deification abhorrent, and Hadrian's very proper successors, Antoninus Pius and Marcus Aurelius, perhaps took no offense at criticisms of the new cult. In the next century, Origen, who as a native of Alexandria in Egypt had local knowledge, affirms that the Antinoites still celebrated mysteries of "the god Antinoos" and that through the art of

Pl. 9. The Obelisk of Antinoos, Rome (courtesy of the American Academy in Rome and Fototeca Unione)

magicians, Antinoos issued "oracles" thought to cure diseases; a magical tablet from Antinooupolis, dated to the third or fourth century, confirms Origen's testimony by showing him as a "divinity of the dead" *(nekyo-daimôn)*, able to bind a woman to her lover. Christian writers are in general fond of using him to show up pagan beliefs as irrational and immoral. Some, such as Hegesippos and Clement, refer only to his cult in Antinooupolis, while others such as Justin Martyr claim that "everyone rushed out of fear to worship him as a god" *(pantes dia phobou hôs theon sebein hôrmênto)*, but this is a manifest exaggeration.[4]

Among cities outside Egypt, a distinction can be drawn between those in which Hadrian's interference is visible or likely, and those that acted more or less spontaneously. In the first group, the leaders are Antinoos' home city of Bithynion and Mantinea in Arcadia, Bithynion's reputed mother-city. For Mantinea there is the witness of Pausanias, writing a generation or so after the institution of the cult. "Antinoos has been regarded *(enomisthê)* as a god, and of the temples in Mantinea the newest is the temple *(naos)* of Antinoos. He was somewhat extraordinarily favored *(perissôs dê ti espoudasthê)* by the emperor Hadrian. I did not see him when he was still among mankind, but I have seen him in cult-statues *(agalmata)* and in pictures *(graphai)*. He has honors *(gera)* elsewhere too, and in the Nile there is a city of the Egyptians named after Antinoos, and he has received honors in Mantinea for the following reason. By birth Antinoos was from Bithynion by the river Sangarios, of which the citizens are Arcadians and Mantineans by origin. For these reasons the emperor (Hadrian) established honors for him in Mantinea too, and there is an annual mystery-rite *(teletê)* and a contest for him every fourth year. There is a room in the gymnasium of the Mantineans containing cult-statues of Antinoos, which beside other properties is remarkable for the marble with which it is adorned and for the pictures on display, most of which show Antinoos made to look very like Dionysos."[5]

Pausanias is correct in saying that Mantinea, where Hadrian was the founder of the cult, regarded Antinoos as a god. An inscription of the city shows that a Spartan aristocrat, Gaius Julius Eurycles Herculanus, also a friend of Plutarch, left money to build a stoa in honor of Mantinea "and of the local god *(epichôrios theos)* Antinoos." A more personal inscription is carved on a column-base destined to hold a statue, probably inside the god's temple. The verse-text shows the subject, Isochrysos, to have been a young man whom "Antinoos the god himself, loving him, raised up to sit with the immortals."[6]

Similar honors appear in Antinoos' home-city of Bithynion, and here too Hadrian must have intervened. A citizen of consular rank acts as priest *(thuêkoos)* of the mysteries of Antinoos, perhaps in the late second century or early third, and on a lower social level a man dedicates an altar to "the new *(or* young) god Antinoos." As at Antinooupolis, there was a prestigious athletic contest, though here it is equal in rank to the Actia founded by Augustus at Nicopolis and is named for Antinoos and Hadrian jointly. The new god also gave his name to one of the tribes of the city, *Antinois,* which followed immediately after *Hadrianê* in the official order.[7]

About thirty cities or leagues of the eastern empire honor Antinoos on their coinage, and the inscriptions and images on these coins add to the information obtainable from literature. Only a few of these sites are in Greece, where coinage in this period is much less abundant than in Asia Minor: Arcadia, Mantinea, Argos, and Corinth in the central or northeastern Peloponnese, Delphi in Phocis, and Nicopolis in Epirus. In Asia Minor there is a concentration in Bithynia, with an outlier at Amisos in Pontus, and a handful of cities in Aeolis, Mysia, and Lydia, with a similar outlier at Amorion in northeastern Phrygia and Tarsos in Cilicia. There are only two from the cultural heartland to the south, Ephesos and Smyrna. This clustering suggests that the cult was often local and spontaneous, and not only the result of imperial pressure.[8]

Antinoos was also commemorated in contests that included both athletic and artistic or "musical" categories, probably competitions in encomium. Beside those of Antinooupolis, Mantinea, and Bithynion, there were lesser, local ones elsewhere. Athens had gymnastic *Antinoeia* both in the city and at Eleusis, in which only ephebes competed; the Eleusinian ones again show the dead youth's assimilation to Iacchos and his role as intermediary between worlds. At Tomis on the Black Sea, the contest honored him as a god, and a leading citizen was the first person to act as president *(agônothetês).* Most or even all of the cities and leagues that honor Antinoos on their coins must have had such contests, similarly patronized by the local nobility, as well as cult-places for his worship, an

open-air sanctuary *(temenos)* or a temple *(neôs)* decorated with his portraits. It can be presumed that the cult-statues *(agalmata)* and pictures
from which the traveler Pausanias knew him stood in such sanctuaries,
and that many of the extant portraits come from the same source; Pausanias cannot have missed the life-size one in Delphi where Antinoos appears in heroic nudity as the "hero before the gates" *(hêrôs propylaios).*[9]

A notable feature of certain coins of Antinoos is that they name the
benefactors who subsidized that issue. At Delphi this person is a priest
called Aristotimos, and one of the coin-types shows the extant statue. He
was a leader of the community, a friend of Plutarch, an ambassador who
represented Delphi before Hadrian in 125, and is identical with "Titus
Flavius Aristotimos the priest" who set up a statue of Hadrian in the same
year. At Corinth a certain Hosterius Marcellus is "priest of Antinoos." The
benefactor Julius Saturninus at Ancyra may well be a governor of the
province. At Smyrna the donor is the wealthy sophist, Antonius Polemo,
whom Hadrian chose to deliver the inaugural speech for the Olympieion
of Athens in 130, the very year of Antinoos' death. It thus appears that
highly placed persons known to Hadrian and knowledgeable about his
wishes promoted the cult in those places where they were influential, thus
providing an impetus for the cult in addition to that of local and regional
devotion. A similar influence may be suspected to explain the presence of
the cult in regional capitals such as Nicopolis in Epirus, Ancyra in Galatia,
and Tarsus in Cilicia.[10]

Almost all the coins describe Antinoos as a hero. Even those of Mantinea, where he was certainly venerated as a god, call him variously both
god and hero. Delphian ones expand the title to "hero before the gates"
(hêrôs propylaios), those of Hadrianoutherai to "good hero" *(hêrôs
agathos).* At Adramyttion he is "Iacchos Antinoos," at Tarsus "new Iacchos"; the title "new" need not suggest that he is identified with the god,
but rather that he incorporates the god's powers and presides over his
own mysteries as Iacchos does at Eleusis. New mystery rites occur frequently in this period; there were even "imperial mysteries" in which
the "Emperor-revealer" *(sebastophantês)* displayed the imperial image to
the initiates. The mysteries of Antinoos presumably had the traditional
function of purifying the souls of the initiates for entrance into the next
life.[11]

Whatever Hadrian's beliefs, Antinoos acquired his own religious aura as a divinity who moved between the three realms of heaven, earth, and the underworld, able like Hermes to give souls safe passage above or below earth. Thus Isochrysos' father at Mantinea imagines him raising his late son to be "seated beside" *(synthronos)* the immortals, and at Rome his "prophet" accords him the same title, "seated beside the gods in Egypt." This role also helps to explain the temple that he shares with Diana at Lanuvium near the goddess's cult site at Aricia, southeast of Rome. This was founded in 133, and then received a generous benefaction from the town's patron in 136. It is not a public temple, but the cult-site of a "college" whose main occupation was to celebrate the festal days of the two divinities and of the human benefactors and to provide proper burial for its members, some of whom are slaves. A famous relief of Antinoos in the guise of Silvanus is also from Lanuvium.[12]

The cult of Antinoos far exceeds the cult of other heroes of the imperial period, whether private or civic, both in geographical spread and in degree of elaboration. No other such hero has mysteries attached to him, or contests in his name, and no other is thought to answer prayers or cure diseases. Nonetheless, the wellspring of the cult of Antinoos is Hadrian's personal loss of his young favorite, and to this extent it differs from other such cults only in scale and not in kind. An emperor is a citizen writ large, and what is personal to him is inevitably public. Those cities that set up their own cults of Antinoos, whether as hero or god, do so either at the emperor's behest or in sympathy with him; highly placed persons with personal links to the emperor promote the cult as an act of respectful consolation. There is no question of official deification by the Roman state, such as is accorded regularly to members of the imperial family as well as to the rulers.

Despite the differences from other such personal cults, there are also similarities. The closest are those founded by Herodes Atticus, though they may show the influence of the emperor's example. Herodes too established a private contest for his dead foster-son Polydeucion, and the poem that he commissioned for Regilla represents her as midway between human and divine. Persons at a humbler level imagine their loved ones carried off to sit in Elysium or seated with the immortals on Olympos. Such loved ones are usually sons, daughters, or occasionally foster-children, but never lovers; similarly, the inscriptions of Antinoos, unlike certain of the literary texts, never refer to him as Hadrian's lover. The inscription on the obelisk in Rome represents him as a god who calls on the god Re-Harakte, a manifestation of the god Horus, as "his father," and asks for his blessing on Hadrian for establishing his cult in Egypt; it goes on to praise the emperor as the "Lord of Welfare, the ruler of every land, the exalted one," while Sabina is "his great consort, beloved by him, the queen of both lands [both Upper and Lower Egypt] and of the cities." Pausanias, the closest in time of non-Christian commentators, uses the expression "was favored," which leaves the relationship ambiguous. Although it may have been widely assumed that Antinoos was the passive partner *(erômenos)* and Hadrian the active *(erastês),* he is in fact a complete blank: no record survives of his human parents, of any interaction with other members of the court, or of any speech or deed. In official art, the only active role in which he is depicted is as Hadrian's companion in his favorite sport of hunting. Besides the celebrated *tondi* now on the Arch of Constantine in Rome, a coin of Hadrianoutherai ("Hadrian's Hunts") in Mysia has on the obverse a bust of Antinoos as "good hero" *(hêrôs agathos),* on the reverse the head of a bear.[13]

This very blankness of Antinoos may have promoted his cult, allowing all varieties of interpretation to be placed upon his memory, and turning him from the constant companion of this much-traveled emperor into an object of veneration. The youth's beauty and early death gave him two of the traditional attributes of heroes, and the fact that this handsome nobody from a small town in Bithynia could become the inseparable partner of the ruler of the Roman Empire could well have added a sense of the miraculous, especially after he had been snatched away under mysterious circumstances and in the bloom of youth. Reinforced by the belief that the young dead, even family members, could become "good heroes" and visit the living in dreams and apparitions, a cult sprang up that became personal for more than the emperor, and lasted down to the fourth century.

In certain ways the growth and rapid spread of the cult of Antinoos resembles a cult that sprang up at almost exactly the same time in another part of the same province, Paphlagonia. Its promoter was not an emperor but Alexander of Abonuteichos, of whom the satirist Lucian has given so partial an account that Alexander's true motives are now impossible to fathom. He began to propagate his new god Glycon, a newborn *(artigennêtos)* Asclepios in the form of a gigantic snake, about the same time as Hadrian began to encourage worship of Antinoos. The cult is especially dense in Glycon's own Paphlagonia and the neighboring Pontus and Bithynia, though it turns up far from its origin in Athens, in Tomis on the Black Sea, and in Dacia. Like the cult of Antinoos, it included mysteries and formed a new focus of religious expectation. Favored by highly placed Romans, including the emperor Marcus Aurelius, the cult of Glycon became a powerful force in the religious life of its native Paphlagonia, and spread its influence far and wide before it too faded away, probably under the pressure of Christianity.[14]

The Roman Empire in its afternoon splendor continues the Hellenistic tradition of civic and familial heroization, of which the posthumous exaltation of Antinoos is the most flagrant example. The first half of the third century is the setting of Philostratus' *Dialog on Heroes,* an equally resplendent monument to the heroes of myth. But two hundred years after Hadrian, after the transforming gulf of the mid-third century, his successor Constantine began to promote a new religion that replaced the diversity of traditional cults with a monotheism that boded ill for the gods of what was now called "Hellenism" or (in the West) "paganism." It remains to see what happened to heroes and the cult of heroes in this last phase of Antiquity.

CHAPTER 8

Heroes and Saints

✦

In the *City of God,* written after the Gothic sack of Rome in 410, Augustine asks why demons have been given the power to persecute the faithful. The reason is that the deaths of martyrs people the City of God with new recruits who have vanquished impiety, and "these we would much more elegantly, if the ecclesiastical mode of speaking allowed it, call our heroes." Augustine explains that Greek myth derived the word "hero" from a supposed son of Hera called Heros, "since the fable signified a secret, as it were, because the air is assigned to Hera, and there they allege that the heroes, a name that they use for the souls of some virtuous men, dwell with the demons." If we could call our martyrs heroes, he continues, we would do so not because they associate with the demons in the air, but because they defeat the demons, who are aerial powers, including Juno, "who is not inappropriately represented by the poets as hostile to virtues and envious towards men who seek heaven." Aeneas indeed had overcome Juno with "suppliant gifts," but "our heroes, if we could properly call them so, defeat Hera not with suppliant gifts but divine virtues."[1]

Augustine's comparison of martyrs with the heroes of epic (which for him means primarily the *Aeneid*) raises a question much debated since the nineteenth century: whether there is a link between the pagan cult of the dead, in particular the cult of heroes, and the Christian cult of the saints. The problem is complicated in several ways. On the side of paganism, the word "hero" denotes the heroes of poetry and myth, including local figures such as the obscure Androcrates of Plataea mentioned in passing by Thucydides, but also the new heroes created by communities and families such as Aurelius Octavius, a "holy and decent man," honored as a hero by Arcesine on Amorgos. On the side of Christianity, the veneration of the ordinary dead is different from the cult of saints. Many of the practices observed by Christians when honoring their dead resemble those of paganism, such as offerings poured through the roof of the tomb and annual commemoration of the departed. The cult of the saints implies much more: reverence for the saint's remains, building of churches and chapels at the saint's grave-site or place of martyrdom, and prayers addressed to the saint.[2]

An extreme form of the argument for continuity between the two types is that certain minor divinities or local heroes survived in the form of saints; some have argued that the early church deliberately fostered such transformations in order to attract pagan converts. Thus Hermann Usener saw a legendary bishop of Amathus in Cyprus, Saint Tychon, as the Christianized form of a fertility god, Tychon; more recently it has been suggested that a young Christian called Nestor, martyred after defeating a gigantic gladiator in the reign of Maximian, is an avatar of the Nestor of Homer. In answer to such constructions, Hippolyte Delehaye observed: "There is no reason to deny the resemblances of detail, or even the analogy of the saints, servants of the true God, and honored by a cult of a lower kind, with the heroes, also like them elevated above humanity, though of a lower rank than the gods. But we should refrain from inferring that the cult of the saints is a derivation from the cult of heroes."[3]

The only heroes that truly survived the advent of Christianity are the earliest ones of Greek literature, especially those of the Homeric poems. The anxieties of early Christianity were fixed on the pagan gods, not on the heroes. The First Commandment enjoined the rejection of other gods, and the story of the Golden Calf illustrated the punishment that awaited those who strayed. The Psalms of David reinforced the lesson: "For all the gods of the pagans are demons *(daimonia)*; but the Lord made the heavens," and "The idols of the pagans are silver and gold, the work of men's hands . . . Those who make them are like them; so are all who trust in them." The apostle Paul reaffirmed such beliefs: "An idol has no real existence," and the gentiles "have served creation rather than the Creator."[4]

In the second century, Christianity moved more deeply into the gentile world, and attracted converts such as Justin Martyr who possessed a profound knowledge of Greek thought and literature. The arguments concerning the objects of pagan worship now become more nuanced, and distinctions start to appear. The gods of the pagans were no longer those of the Canaanites and the Philistines, but ones familiar to every Greek and Roman, and it was not so easy to condemn the Zeus of Homer and Pheidias as to condemn Baal or Moloch. These more Hellenized Christians continued to observe the Pauline anathema on pagan idols, on the food sacrificed to them, and on the rites surrounding the worship of pagan gods. Yet it became a question whether these gods had actually existed in some past time, if so whether they were identical with the demons, and whether those who had written about them were entirely devoid of light.

For Justin Martyr, one of the earliest of the Christian apologists, the sins that the Greeks ascribed to gods such as adultery and pederasty were actually committed by demons. When Socrates tried to discourage worship of these demons, they caused him to be put to death. Justin can even affirm that the Christian doctrine of Jesus as the Son of God has its analogy in Greek accounts of "those whom you call sons of Zeus," such as Hermes, Asclepius, Heracles, and Perseus. The difference from the Christian Logos was that pagan writers represented such heroes as the sons of gods "for the advantage and the instruction of students, since all agree that it is noble to imitate the gods." By contrast, the stories told about Zeus himself, his love affairs with Ganymede and countless women, were the invention of demons. The same demons knew that David and the Prophets foretold the coming of Christ, but did not fully understand their meaning. Hence "they produced many who were reputed to be the sons of Zeus, thinking that they would sow a suspicion in men's mind that the things foretold of Christ were a fable and similar to the sayings of poets." The demons then took care that these poems should become known throughout the world in order to forestall belief in the divinity of Christ. Thus by arguing that only demons had turned human benefactors such as Asclepius and Heracles into supposed sons of Zeus, Justin goes far to rescue them from Christian condemnation and to exempt them from the prohibition on worshiping other gods.[5]

Tatian, the author of an extant *Address to the Greeks,* is a contemporary of Justin, and like him a convert from paganism. He too holds that the pagan gods are demons in disguise, but is even more indulgent than Justin towards heroes. After giving a vivid account of the kind of stage-artist that the Greeks called a "dancer" *(orchêstês)*, the Romans a "pantomime," Tatian calls one that he had witnessed "an accuser of all the gods, an epitome of superstition, a disparager of heroism" *(diabolos hêrôikôn praxeôn)*. He appears to mean that the mythological ballets that formed the repertory of such dancers, by representing such subjects as the love-affair of Ares and Aphrodite or the madness of Ajax, "accused" the gods by recalling their immoral actions but "disparaged" the heroes by enacting their bad deeds rather then their good ones. Elsewhere Tatian uses the heroes to rebut the contention that Christians imparted their doctrines to the very young. "Achilles was a young man and is believed to have had true nobility; Neoptolemos was younger, but strong; Philoctetes was ill, but heaven *(to daimonion)* needed him against Troy."[6]

A treatise erroneously attributed to Justin Martyr, the *Exhortation to the Greeks,* is actually by an unknown author writing a century or so later. Like other apologists, he uses Homer's account of the gods to argue that either they do not exist, or if they did they were not gods. But he goes further, and supposes that the poet had an inkling of the Jewish scriptures, having inspected them during a visit to Egypt, and he shows his acceptance of their truths by subtle hints. Thus the famous half-line "Many masters are no good thing" *(ouk agathon polukoiraniê)* is a veiled affirmation of monotheism; the account of Achilles' shield shows his knowledge of the story of Creation; his description of the Palace of Alcinoos, with its abundance of plants and flowers, reveals his knowledge of Paradise.[7]

The way was open for a further step, towards giving the title of "hero" to Christians of extraordinary excellence. Although Augustine considered this outside "the ecclesiastical mode of speech," secular writers were under no such constraint. Thus Prudentius, after praising the feats of John the Evangelist, whom he identifies with the author of the Apocalypse, imagines him sleeping the sleep of the virtuous: "in such sleep the just hero refreshes his mind," *tali sopore iustus mentem relaxat heros.* Greek verse-inscriptions similarly call their Christian subjects "heroes," though qualifying them with epic-sounding adjectives such as "most-excellent" *(polyesthlos)* and "right-renowned" *(agakleitos).* Even the emperor Anastasius could be honored as a "great-named hero" *(megalônumos hêrôs)* for restoring a bathhouse in Palestine. A long verse poem on a general called Constantius is now known only from manuscript copies. Though the subject is presumably a Christian, the opening lines present him as a warrior-hero of classic type:

> Hic decus Italiae tegitur, Constantius heros,
> Qui patriae tegimen, murus et arma fuit.
> Invictus bello, non fictae pacis amator,
> Confixus plagis, victor ubique tamen.

[Here lies the glory of Italy, the hero Constantius, who was the shield, wall and arms of his fatherland. Invincible in war, no lover of feigned peace, pierced with wounds, but yet victorious everywhere.][8]

After the conversion of Constantine to Christianity and the beginning of restrictions on pagan practices, the old believers continued to worship the traditional heroes, though with growing caution. The emperor Julian writes to an unnamed pagan priest to justify his favor to a certain Pegasius, who had been bishop of Alexandria Troas, and recounts an experience from a time when he was still Caesar and supposedly Christian. Visiting the nearby Ilion with Pegasius as his guide, Julian toured the memorials of the Trojan War.

> Hector has a hero's shrine *(hêrôon)* there and his bronze portrait-statue *(andrias)* stands in a tiny little temple. Opposite this they have set up the great Achilles in the unroofed court . . . Now I found that the altars were still alight, I might almost say still blazing, and that the statue of Hector had been anointed till it shone. So I looked at Pegasius and said: "What does this mean? Do the people of Ilion offer sacrifices?" This was to test him cautiously to find out his own views. He replied: "Is it not natural that they should worship a noble man who was their own citizen, just as we worship the martyrs?" Now the analogy *(eikôn)* was not sound *(hygiês)*; but his point of view and intentions were those of a man of culture, if you consider the times in which we then lived. Observe what followed. "Let us go," said he, "to the shrine of Athena of Ilion." Immediately with the greatest eagerness he led me there and opened the temple, and as though he were

> producing evidence he showed me all the cult-statues *(agalmata)* in
> perfect preservation . . . This same Pegasius went with me to the tem-
> ple of Achilles *(Achilleion)* as well and showed me the tomb in good
> repair; yet I had been informed that he had reduced this to ruins too.
> But he approached it with great reverence, as I saw with my own eyes.

Julian intends by his letter to clear Pegasius from the suspicion of an insincere paganism, and perhaps to justify himself for appointing him as a pagan priest, but the outcome is unknown.[9]

In 375, twelve years after Julian's death, a pagan priest of Athens invoked the aid of Achilles. This was Nestorius, the hierophant or "sacred revealer" of the Mysteries of Demeter at Eleusis. He had long ago initiated Julian into the Mysteries, and now, when Greece was being ravaged by earthquakes, he had a dream ordering him to honor Achilles at public expense. He communicated the message to the Athenian authorities, who ignored him as a senile driveller, whereupon, according to the historian Zosimus, "he created an image of the hero in a miniature temple and placed it at the foot of the statue of Athena standing in the Parthenon, and while carrying out the customary rites for the goddess he also accomplished for the hero what was laid down for him according to tradition." Thus Athens alone was spared from the earthquake, "and all of Attica participated in the hero's benefactions." In the next century, the Neoplatonist philosopher Syrianus commemorated this exploit in a hymn, whence it passed into Zosimus' history, a vivid example of the persistence of the pagan faith in heroes well into Late Antiquity.[10]

A pagan "high-priest" *(archiereus)* called Helladius known from an inscription of Megara provides an analogy to Pegasius at Ilion and Nestorius in Athens. An epigram attributed to Simonides and honoring "those heroes who died in the Persian War and who lie here" had become faint, and Helladius had it reinscribed, writing at the end of the text, "Up to our day the city sacrifices [or: used to sacrifice, *enagizen*] a bull." Interpreters are divided whether to take the verb in the present or the imperfect tense; if the imperfect is right, sacrifice had perhaps been discontinued because of the fear of Christian authorities.[11]

Julian's observation on the "unsoundness" of Pegasius' analogy arises from the belief, often expressed by fourth-century pagans, that the cult of martyrs was morbid and impious, a gruesome attachment to bodily remains and burial-places, whereas the cult of heroes implied a reverence for personal excellence and manly bravery. Shrines such as that of Protesilaos in Elaious or of Achilles in Ilion could stand near the hero's burial-place, but to introduce the hero's remains into the actual shrine would have been an act of impiety. Hence in Julian's reign as emperor arose the scandal of the remains of St. Babylas at Antioch: by moving the martyr's relics to Daphne, Julian's brother Gallus had caused the oracle of Apollo to fall silent. Julian duly sent the relics back to Antioch, but the Temple of Apollo at Daphne burned shortly afterwards.[12]

Whereas Julian attempted to prevent Christian teachers from teaching the pagan classics, Christian emperors, though they destroyed pagan temples and anti-Christian literature, left those same classics unharmed. Christians accepted the view of Plutarch and other educators that the poems of Homer and Hesiod were not dangerous, provided that teachers and students knew how to extract lessons of virtue from them; this is the essential message of Basil of Caesarea's influential *Address to Young Men on Reading Pagan Literature.* A sophisticated Christian could think in two realms, one of his religious belief, the other of his classical education, and the classical heroes were all the more innocuous since, as Augustine observed, "hero" was a word that pagans had used "for the souls of some virtuous men."[13]

Some time about the year 400, the bereaved husband of a young woman called Eustathia commemorated her with an inscribed gravestone, setting it up in a Christian basilica of Demetrias in Thessaly. She had belonged to a noble family of the city, and the monument bore a poem of ten very faulty hexameters, the meter called "heroic" from its association with the poems of Homer. It begins: "O stranger, do not wonder what mortal lies here. It is my Eustathia, about whom everyone knows who she is. If you too wish to know of what family and what origin she is, she is (descended) from Aeacides, whose family is the first *(hou genos esti to prôton)."* Readers would have recognized behind the name "Aeacides" either Peleus, the son of Aeacus and husband of the sea-goddess Thetis, or more probably their son Achilles, and they would have been all the more alert to the allusion since their city was the successor of the prehistoric Iolcos, which according to legend Peleus had conquered and had attached to Thessaly. Thus Eu-

Pl. 10. Detail of silver plate showing Achilles, Augst (courtesy of AUGUSTA RAURICA, Augst)

stathia, this young Christian wife, was descended from Achilles, the son of a sea-goddess, and her husband was glad to commemorate her heroic ancestry when burying her in a Christian basilica.[14]

Achilles, Eustathia's distant ancestor, is a favorite subject in the art of Late Antiquity. A silver plate discovered at Kaiseraugst in 1961 and dated to the fourth century has ten scenes round the rim illustrating Achilles' childhood; in the center a tondo shows a famous incident of his youth, Odysseus' discovery of him on the island of Scyros (Pl. 10). According to the myth, Thetis had hidden him there disguised as a girl in order to prevent him sailing to Troy, where she knew that he would be killed. The Greeks, knowing that his presence was indispensable for their victory, sent Odysseus disguised as a merchant to the island, and with him a trumpeter. When Odysseus brought out weapons from among his wares, and the trumpeter blew a battle-signal, Achilles broke through his disguise and Thetis' plan was frustrated. The tondo shows Deidameia, the local princess with whom Achilles had fallen in love, trying to restrain him, the hero pulling away from her, Odysseus pointing in the direction of Troy, and the trumpeter blowing the signal. It has been rightly argued that this series of scenes, with their climax in the central tondo, "marks not only the end of Achilles' childhood but also the end of the false path that has been leading him away from his true destiny as a warrior." If that is right, here again it is Achilles as an exemplar of military virtue that interests the Late Antique viewer. The same scene in a slightly different form appears in the central tondo of the Achilles Plate that is part of the so-called Sevso Treasure. Here the scenes around the rim include Achilles' first bath, while the other scenes are unconnected with him.[15]

Christian thinkers admired Achilles, Hector, and others like them without making them imaginary beings who had never lived in the real world. They did not turn them into Christians before Christianity, as they sometimes did with Socrates, Vergil, or Seneca. Instead they found a way to accept their exceptional status without compromising their belief that only one person had truly combined the human and the divine, that only He was the Son of God and not one of several sons of God. Though to us culture might seem a less powerful force for unity than religion or nationality, in fact it served to provide cohesion across the barriers that time was constantly erecting in the Mediterranean world. In the fourth century, when Christianity appeared to add the barrier of religion, Greek culture gave its own kind of blood to the hardiest of Greek heroes, the heroes of epic and myth.

Appendix: Living Heroes?

✦

Erwin Rohde in *Psyche,* his classic and often reprinted study of ancient ideas of death and the afterlife, gave powerful impetus to the view that heroism had "degenerated" in postclassical times. One of his arguments ran as follows: "It became a custom followed almost unthinkingly to mark even private persons with the title of hero in their lifetime, to confer heroic honors, and even the foundation of annually recurring competitions, on living people." The "debased hellenistic habit of according 'heroic' honors to the living," as it has been called, has been traced even to the fifth century.[1]

Rohde started from an observation that Théodore Reinach made in 1890 concerning the city of Cyzicus in Mysia, which dated its years by the annual "hipparch." Publishing an inscription of Cyzicus dated to the year of "Claudius Eteoneus, hero," Reinach commented: "The eponymous hipparch carries the title of *hêrôs* which is frequently given to men and women in the epigraphy of Cyzicus, even in their lifetime."[2] A few years after Reinach, in 1896, the great epigraphist Adolf Wilhelm discussed the practice of Greek cities whereby a person gave an endowment to underwrite an office essential to community life. If there was a vacancy, whether because no one had offered to undertake the office or for some other reason, the benefactor was considered the "eternal" *(aiônios)* or "continuous" *(diênekês)* holder of the office, while the actual duties were performed by a substitute. The position most frequently funded in this way is that of the gymnasiarch, who defrayed the cost of supplying the public gymnasia with olive oil, while other foundations supported eponymous magistracies. An inscription from Larisa in Asian Aeolis envisages this very situation: a man who has been gymnasiarch four times gives certain estates to his city "in order that from (the income of) the estates he may be gymnasiarch for eternity."[3]

Although Wilhelm did not explicitly address cases in which the office-holder was a hero or heroine, Louis Robert has drawn the obvious inference that such a person held the position posthumously by virtue of a foundation made in his or her lifetime. A series of letters written by the emperor Hadrian to Aphrodisias in Caria is dated by the eponymous magistrate of the city, the "crown-wearer" *(stephanêphoros)*, as well as by the emperor's titles. In one letter, the magistrate is called "Tiberius Claudius Hypsicles," whereas in one only slightly later he is "Claudius Hypsicles, hero," and had therefore died in the interim. The hipparchy of Cyzicus must have been endowed in the same way as the office of "crown-wearer" at Aphrodisias, and there is no reason to assume with Reinach that the heroes and heroines who held the position did so in their lifetimes.[4]

While Reinach's examples can thus be discounted, it is not impossible that "heroic" honors were sometimes bestowed on the living, even though the association of heroes with the next world might have seemed as ill-omened as when an obscure Roman senator thought to flatter Nero by giving him the title *divus* ("deified") "as having surpassed mortal level and deserving of veneration from humans." Apart from the instances of Hagnon at Amphipolis and the athlete Euthymos discussed above, the following are the most plausible examples of such living heroes.[5]

1. According to Diodorus Siculus, the people of Syracuse rewarded Dion, their liberator from the tyranny of Dionysius II, by electing him general with full powers and granting him "heroic honors" *(hêrôikai timai)*. When speaking of an earlier champion of Syracuse, Diocles, Diodorus uses the same expression but adds a past participle, "after his death" *(teleutêsanta),* and his omission of the participle here might imply that Dion received these honors while still alive. Yet this may be an early instance of a practice frequent in the historian's own day, the voting of honors in anticipation of a person's death. Such anticipatory honors usually involve the honorand's funeral and burial, for example, permission for him to be buried within the city. The most conspicuous instance is Diodoros Pasparos of Pergamon a generation or so before Diodorus

Siculus. Already in his lifetime his fellow-citizens voted to name a tribe after him, the "Paspareïs," to institute a priest for him "as for the other benefactors," and to establish a sacred area *(temenos)* called the *Diodoreion* with a temple and cult-statue *(agalma);* when he died he was to be buried in one of the agoras of the city. It can hardly be doubted that after his death Diodoros became a local hero.[6]

2. Demochares, the nephew of Demosthenes and an avowed opponent of Macedonian rule over Athens, was also a historian, and Athenaeus quotes him as describing the disgraceful flattery shown by the Athenians towards the Macedonian king, Demetrios Poliorcetes, in 302. They honored two of the king's mistresses, Lais and Leaina, with sanctuaries *(hiera)*, and three of his "flatterers" *(kolakes)*, Bourichos, Adeimantos, and Oxythemis, with "altars, *hêrôa* and libations, and paeans were sung to each of them, so that Demetrios himself wondered at these happenings, and said that in his time no Athenian existed who was great and fine of soul." Of these three "flatterers," inscriptions show that Adeimantos had a major position as the Macedonian representative in Greece, and that the Athenians honored both him and Oxythemis with laudatory decrees. It is certain that they sang paeans to Demetrios and his father Antigonos the One-Eyed, and a celebrated Athenian hymn in honor of Demetrios, written by a certain Hermocles some twelve years later, is still extant; in this he is explicitly called a god and the son of Poseidon and Aphrodite. Though Demochares does not say that the "altars, *hêrôa* and libations" were for the veneration of the three Macedonian officials in their lifetime, that is the natural reading of the text. But it is also possible that, as one who had every motive to exaggerate the flattery of his pro-Macedonian opponents, he has given a deliberately misleading account, and that some of these honors were voted in anticipation, like those for Diodoros Pasparos.[7]

3. During the last years of the Roman republic, a literary man with powerful friends at Rome, Nicias of Cos, established a "tyranny" over his fellow-citizens that lasted at least eight years. A number of dedications invoke the city's ancestral gods "for the safety *(sôtêria)* of Nicias, son of the People, lover of his ancestral land *(patris)*, hero, benefactor of the city." The language strongly suggests that Nicias is among the living, though it does not indicate whether his "safety" has to do with his health, for example, his recovery from an illness, or with something such as his

return from a dangerous journey. This exception is to be explained by Nicias' dominance of his community: as a person of extraordinary power in his city and of wide influence at Rome, he had extorted from his subjects a title usually reserved for the virtuous dead. A person dominant in Cos a hundred years later, Claudius' doctor Xenophon, may also have been a living hero, though the evidence is more ambiguous.[8]

There appear to be no further examples of "living" heroes. Diodorus Siculus several times refers to persons fighting or dying "heroically" (*hêrôikôs*) on the battlefield, and Cicero half-ironically refers to the Younger Cato as *heros ille noster*, "our doughty champion," for his vigorous performance in the senate, but these are not exceptions. In Late Antiquity, Eusebius applies "hero" ironically to Apollonius of Tyana, and Julian does so sincerely to Iamblichus, but in both instances the word refers to persons long dead and means simply "the great."[9]

Notes

Index

Notes

Syll.[3]   *Sylloge Inscriptionum Graecarum,* 3rd edition

TAM   *Tituli Asiae Minoris*

ZPE   *Zeitschrift für Papyrologie und Epigraphik*

1. Poetic Heroes

1. *Il.* 1.1–4 (my translation). Translators such as A. T. Murray and William F. Wyatt in the LCL render *hêrôôn* as "warriors," but see further below.

2. Herodotus: 2.53.Z, (trans. A. D. Godley, LCL). I assume the commonly accepted dates of ca. 750 for the writing down of the *Iliad,* 725 for the *Odyssey,* 700 for Hesiod, but make no assumption about the nature or stages of "composition." The meaning of the word "hero" in the archaic period, and in particular whether the cult of heroes derives from ancestor-worship *(Ahnenkult),* is debated: see an accessible recent overview by A. Mazarakis Ainian in *Thesaurus Cultus and Rituum antiquorum* 2 (Los Angeles, 2004) 131–134.

3. Meaning of *hêrôs*: Istros, *FGrHist* 334 F 69 (kings only); Apollon. Soph., *Lex. Hom.* p. 84.22 Bekker ("all who lived in those times"). Plato: *Cra.* 398 C-D *(erôs, eirein),* August. *Civ. Dei* 10.21 (Hera). Modern discussions include S. Eitrem, art. "Heros," *RE* 8 (1912) 1111; Ian Morris, *Archaeology as Cultural History: Words and Things in Iron-Age Greece* (Malden, Mass., 2000) 253; A. Mazarakis Ainian (previous n.).

4. *Tiriseroe:* Michael Ventris and John Chadwick, *Documents in Mycenaean Greek*[2] (Cambridge, Eng., 1973) 286–289 no. 172.

5. *Oxford English Dictionary* 6.442.

6. *Od.* 6.303 (Alcinoos), 11.342 (Echeneos, Phaeacian elder), 15.117 (Phaidimos king of Sidon), 8.483 (Demodocos bard). Thus Arthur D. Nock, "The Cult of Heroes," *Essays in Religion and the Ancient World* (Cambridge, Mass., 1972) 2.595, "the word itself was once a term of respect, like *kyrios, dominus,* Messire, my lord."

7. Wives and daughters: *Od.* 11.329. Menelaus: *Od.* 4.561–569 (my translation).

8. For the view of Homeric influence, see especially John N. Coldstream, "Hero-Cults in the Age of Homer," *JHS* 96 (1976) 8–17.

9. *Od.* 10.516–529, 11.23–36. For *melikrêton,* Paul Stengel, *Opferbräuche der Griechen* (Leipzig and Berlin, 1910) 180, 186. On *enagismos,* below, ch. 2.

10. Hesiod on the five races: *Op.* 106–201, especially 167–173 on the "fourth race" (all translations by Glenn L. Most, LCL).

11. *Catalogue of Women:* essential discussion by Martin L. West, *The Hesiodic Catalogue of Women* (Oxford, 1985) especially 1 (on the various titles), 118–121 (the Helen episode and the snake); text in Glenn W. Most, *Hesiod:* The Shield, Cat-

alogue of Women, *Other Fragments* (Cambridge, Mass., 2007) 40–277; on the ending of the poem, Jenny S. Clay, "The Beginning and the Ending of the *Catalogue of Women* and Its Relation to Hesiod," in Richard Hunter, ed., *The Hesiodic* Catalogue of Women (Cambridge, Eng., 2005), 25–34. Julia daughter of Nicias: Ernst Pfuhl and Hans Möbius, *Die Ostgriechischen Grabreliefs* 2 (Mainz am Rhein, 1977/1979) no. 2088 with pl. 301 (Peek, *Griechische Vers-Inschriften* 438a).

12. "Plataea poem": text in Martin L. West, *Iambi et Elegi Graeci* [2] (Oxford, 1992) 118–122; revised text and translation by David Sider in Deborah Boedeker and David Sider, *The New Simonides: Contexts of Praise and Desire* (Oxford, 2001) 13–29; on possible intimations of the heroization of contemporaries, Boedeker, "Paths to Heroization at Plataea," in Boedeker and Sider, 148–163; for a skeptical view, Jan M. Bremmer, "The Rise of the Hero Cult and the New Simonides," *ZPE* 158 (2006) 15–26.

13. "What god, what hero, what man?": *Ol.* 2.1. "Hero god": *Nem.* 3.23. Heracles on Olympus: *Isthm.* 4.58–60. Double Heracles: Hdt. 2.44.5.

14. Pelops: *Ol.* 1.90 (trans. Race); for *haimakouria,* in which the second element is connected with the verb *korennumi,* "satisfy," "regale," Pierre Chantraine, *Dictionnaire étymologique de la Langue grecque*[2] (Paris, 1999) 34. Neoptolemos: *Nem.* 7. 43–46. Heracles: *Isthm.* 4.61–66. Protesilaus: *Isthm.* 1.58. Lesser Ajax: *Ol.* 9. 112–113. Tlepolemos: Hom. *Il.* 2.653–670, Pind. *Ol.* 7.77–81.

15. Son of Apollo and Cyrene: *Pyth.* 9.63. Diomedes: *Nem.* 10.8. "Path of Zeus": *Ol.* 2.68–71. Achilles' lament: *Od.* 11.488–491.

16. Pl. *Meno* 81B = Pindar fr. 133 Race (I have slightly modified Race's translation), with the discussion of Günther Zuntz, *Persephone* (Oxford, Eng., 1971) 85–87 and the commentaries on the *Meno* of R. S. Bluck (Cambridge, Eng., 1961) and R. W. Sharples (Warminster, Eng., and Chicago, Ill., 1985).

17. Pindar, *Pyth.* 11.7. Androclea and Alcis: Paus. 9.17.1.

18. Euphamos and Battos: *Pyth.* 4.21–61, 254–261, with the commentary of Bruce K. Braswell (Berlin and New York, 1988); on the Cyrenaean background, François Chamoux, *Cyrène sous la Monarchie des Battiades* (Paris, 1953) ch. 2, "La Colonisation légendaire." Battos' tomb: *Pyth.* 5.89–103, tr. Race (slightly altered).

19. Tomb: Sandro Stucchi, *L'Agora di Cirene I: I Lati nord et est della Platea inferiore* (Rome, 1965) 58–65, 111–114. Catullus: 7.6.

2. Local Heroes

1. Androcrates: Thuc. 3.24.1; Hdt. 9.25.3; Plut. *Aristides* 11. "Little local deities": Arthur D. Nock, "The Cult of Heroes," *Essays in Religion and the Ancient World* (Cambridge, Mass., 1972) 2.593.

2. Protesilaos: Fulvio Canciani, art. "Protesilaos," *LIMC* 7 (1994) 554–560; below, ch. 6.

3. *Od.* 13.13–14, 345–350, 362–365; Sylvia Benton, "Excavations in Ithaca III," *Papers of the British School at Athens* 35 (1934–1935) 45–73; John N. Coldstream, "Hero-Cults in the Age of Homer," *JHS* 96 (1976) 16–17 (in favor); Carla M. Antonaccio, *An Archaeology of Ancestors: Tomb Cult and Hero Cult in Early Greece* (Lanham, Md., 1995) 152–155 (skeptical). Dedication: *IG* 9.1² 4, 1615.

4. Therapne: Sam Wide, *Lakonische Kulte* (Leipzig, 1893) 340–346; Antonaccio, *Archaeology of Ancestors* 165–166. Achilles: Wide, *Lakonische Kulte* 232–238.

5. Chrysapha relief: Manolis Andronikos, "Lakonika Anaglupha," *Peloponnesiaka* 1 (1956) 257–260 with pl. 2; Martin Robertson, *History of Greek Art* (Cambridge, Eng., 1975) 114, 634 n. 92. Snakes: see now Gina Salapata, "Hero Warriors from Corinth and Laconia," *Hesperia* 66 (1997) 249–252; below, ch. 6. Chilon relief: Alan J. B. Wace, "A Spartan Hero Relief," *Archaiologikê Ephemeris* 1937, 217–220, cf. Andronikos, "Lakonika anaglupha" 264, and for the inscription *IG* 5.1, 244. *Hêrôon:* Paus. 3.16.4, with the commentary of Domenico Musti and Mario Torelli (Milan, 1991) 234.

6. Thera: Charalampos Sigalas and Angelos Matthaiou, "Enepigrapha Ostraka apo to Heroon tou Achilleos sten Thera," *Horos* 14–16 (2000–2003) 259–268. Tarentum: Polyb. 8.28.6–8.

7. Selinous tablet: Michael H. Jameson, David R. Jordan, Roy D. Kotansky, *A lex sacra from Selinous, GRBS Monographs* 11 (Durham, N.C., 1993); *SEG* 43.630; Laurent Dubois, *Bull. ép.* 1995, 692, pp. 556–562. Blood through roof of tomb: Paus. 10.4.10 (Daulis in Phocis). *Katagizein:* Michel Casabona, *Recherches sur le Vocabulaire des Sacrifices en Grec* (Aix-en-Provence, 1966) 200–204. *agos:* Gunnel Ekroth, *The Sacrificial Rituals of Greek Hero-Cults* (Liège, 2002) 264–265.

8. *Enagizein:* Nock, "The Cult of Heroes," 591–592, "the tabooing of an animal or removal of it from the secular sphere" (though the word is not confined to animal sacrifice); Casabona, *Recherches* 207–210; Robert Parker, *Miasma* (Oxford, 1983) 328–329; Ekroth, *Sacrificial Rituals* 74–128 (the fullest discussion). Herodotus on Heracles: 2.44.5. The classic demonstration of the blurring between heroic and divine sacrifice is due to Nock, "Cult of Heroes" 576–582.

9. Erechtheus in the Iliad: *Il.* 2.547–551 (trans. Augustus T. Murray and William F. Wyatt, LCL). As represented in Euripides: *Erechtheus* fr. 22, 90–91 (trans. Christopher Collard and Martin Cropp). In general, Ute Kron, art. "Erechtheus," *LIMC* 4.923–927; Emily Kearns, *The Heroes of Attica, BICS* Suppl. 57 (London, 1989), 113–115, 210–211; Antonaccio, *Archaeology of Ancestors* 145 n. 1. Erechtheion: John Travlos, *Pictorial Dictionary of Ancient Athens* (London, 1971) 213–227.

10. In fact the term "hero" is not attested for these figures, or for the Cleisthenic heroes, before Herodotus: but it would be pedantic to use a circumlocution such as "divinized superhuman."

11. Ten Heroes: Hdt. 5.66.2, Arist. *Ath. Pol.* 21.6, 53.4 with the commentary of Peter J. Rhodes; Paus. 1.5.2–4; Kearns, *Heroes* 80–92. Separate worship of tribes: Kearns, *Heroes* 92–101.

12. Arthur Milchhöfer, art. "Butadai," *RE* 3 (1897) 1078; Konrad Wernicke, art. "Butes 1," ib. 1080–1081; Kearns, *Heroes* 152–153.

13. Civic calendar: Franciszek Sokolowski, *Lois sacrées des Cités grecques* (Paris, 1969) no. 1; *IG* 1.1³, 234. Local calendar: Sokolowski, *Lois sacrées* no. 2; *IG* 1³ 234.

14. Inventory: *SEG* 29 (1979) 146. Inscription of Egretes: *IG* 2/3², 2499, 24–30; *Syll.*³ 1097; Sokolowski, *Lois Sacrées* no. 47. Reliefs: Rhea Thönges-Stringaris, "Das Griechische Totenmahl," *Athenische Mitteilungen* 80 (1965) 48–52.

15. W. G. Arnott, *Menander* 2.1–47 (LCL).

16. College of *hêrôstai: IG* 2/3.1339 (57/56).

3. Warriors and Patriots

1. Battos: ch. 1 at n. 18. Miltiades the Elder: Hdt. 6.34–38.1, with the discussion of Irad Malkin, *Religion and Colonization in Ancient Greece* (Leiden, 1987) 190–193. A later Miltiades was sent out to the Adriatic as *oikistês* in 325/24: *IG* 2/3² 1629, 18–19. Brasidas: below. *Thuein:* Michel Casabona, *Recherches sur le Vocabulaire des Sacrifices en Grec* (Aix-en-Provence, 1966) ch. 3, especially 85, "*Thuô* est un terme très général pouvant s'appliquer aussi bien à des sacrifices aux dieux 'd'en-haut' qu'à des offrandes aux héros . . . Mais par opposition à *enagizô*, terme technique désignant les honneurs funèbres rendus aux morts, *thuô* prend la valeur de 'sacrifier à un immortel ou à un dieu Olympien.' "

2. Philippos: Hdt. 5.47. Cf. the Acanthians of Thrace worshiping the very tall Persian, Artachaies, "as a hero," Hdt. 7.117.

3. Honors to descendants: *IG* I² 77 = I³ 131, lines 5-9 (440-432?), Isaeus 5.47, Deinarchus 1.101.

4. Transl. David A. Campbell, *Greek Lyric* V no. 894 (LCL).

5. Restoration in 477/76: *FGrHist* 239 A 54 (*Marmor Parium*). Monument in Agora: Homer A. Thompson and Richard E. Wycherley, *The Athenian Agora* 14: *The Agora of Athens* (Princeton, N.J., 1972) 155–160. Burial-place in Kerameikos: Paus. 1.29.15; John Travlos, *Pictorial Dictionary of Ancient Athens* (New York, 1971) 299–303. *Enagisma*: Aristotle, *Ath. pol.* 58.1.

6. Thuc. 5.11.1 (my translation). It is disputed whether the "pleasure" of the last phrase is the Amphipolitans' or Hagnon's, but the question is only of importance here if Hagnon was dead at the time (see below).

7. *Entemnein:* Casabona, *Recherches* 203–207, citing the scholiast to Thuc. 5.11.1, "because the heads of sacrificial victims are cut off into the earth [this is not

exact]; for this is how they sacrifice to those below *(tois chthoniois)*"; Gunnel Ekroth, *The Sacrificial Rituals of Greek Hero-Cults* (Liège, 2002), 184–185.

8. Athens: Cicero, *Ad fam.* 4.12.3. Burial within city: Sir James Frazer, *Pausanias's Description of Greece* 2 (London, 1898) 533; Eitrem, art. "Heros," *RE* 8 (1912) 1119–1122.

9. *Timê:* Pierre Chantraine, *Dictionnaire étymologique de la Langue grecque²* (Paris, 1999) 1120, "Tout le champ sémantique de *timê* est centré sur la notion de 'prix, valeur.' "

10. "The edifices of Hagnon": Charles F. Smith, *Thucydides* 3.23 (LCL). Buildings named after the founder: Gomme, *Historical Commentary on Thucydides* 3.655. Buildings for the cult of the living Hagnon: Simon Hornblower, *A Commentary on Thucydides* I (Oxford, 1991) 453–455; Bruno Currie, *Pindar and the Cult of Heroes* (Oxford, 2005) 164–166. Herodotus: 5.67.4. Buildings in Athens: Thuc. 2.11.3.

11. A. D. Nock, "*Soter* and *Euergetes*," *Essays on Religion* 2.720, "*Soter* . . . could be used of men and gods alike, and when applied to the latter, it did not necessarily suggest that they belonged or approximated to the category of the former."

12. Burial on the battlefield: Thuc. 2.34.5; Paus. 1.29.4, 32.4 (ghosts). For this interpretation of the horsemen in the Parthenon frieze, John Boardman, "The Parthenon Frieze: Another View," in Ursula Höckmann and Antje Krug, editors, *Festschrift für Frank Brommer* (Mainz, 1977) 43–45.

13. Sacrifice after the battle: Thuc. 2.71.2. Institution of the *Eleutheria:* Diod. Sic. 11.29.1–2, Plut. *Arist.* 21.1–2. I follow the reconstruction of Robert Etienne and Marcel Piérart, "Un Décret du *koinon* des Hellènes à Platées," *BCH* 99 (1975) 63–68.

14. Plataean celebration: Thuc. 3.58.4; Plut. *Aristid.* 21.3–6, with the commentary of Ida Calabi Limentani (Florence, 1966). For *haimakouria,* ch. 1 at n. 14.

15. Funeral oration: Thuc. 2.34. On the problem of the date of this law, Gomme, *A Historical Commentary on Thucydides* 2.4–101; Hornblower, *Commentary* 292–293.

16. On these orations, Gaston Colin, "L'Oraison funèbre d'Hypéride," *REG* 51 (1938) 209–266, is still valuable: more recently, Stephen Usher, *Greek Oratory: Tradition and Originality* (Oxford, 1999) esp. ch. 11, "Ceremonial Oratory." For a defense of the authenticity of the Demosthenic oration, Ian Worthington, *Museum Helveticum* 60 (2003) 152–157.

17. Lys. 2.80; [Demosth.], *Epitaph.* 9, 34. In Isocrates' *Plataean Oration* (60–62), the heroes of Plataea are those to whom the combined Greek forces sacrificed before the battle, not the spirits of those who fell.

18. Arr. *Anab.* 7.14.7. On this passage, Christian Habicht, *Gottmenschentum und griechische Städte²* (Munich, 1970) 29–36.

19. Hyper. *Epitaph.* 21, 35, 39; text in J. O. Burtt, ed., *Minor Attic Orators* 2.532–539 (LCL), whose version I have adapted, also giving the presumed sense of some passages corrupt in the Greek. For a good discussion, Usher, *Greek Oratory* 335–337.

20. Jean Pouilloux, *Recherches sur l'histoire et les cultes de Thasos* I (Paris, 1954) 371–380 no. 141, on which see Ekroth, *Sacrificial Rituals* 135–136. Cf. the "Memorial of the Valiant" *(mnêma tôn Aristeôn)* at Heraclea on the Pontus: Memnon, *FGrHist* 434 F 9 (p. 353, 35).

21. Xen. *Hell.* 7.3.13 (trans. Carleton S. Brownson, LCL, with some alterations). On him, Sian Lewis, "Xenophon's Account of Euphron of Sicyon," *JHS* 124 (2004) 65–74, esp. 71–72 on his burial and cult.

22. For Timoleon's last honors, Diod. Sic. 16.90.1, cf. 19.6.4; Corn. Nep. 20.5.4; Plut. *Tim.* 39.6.

23. Polyb. 12.23.4 = *FGrHist* 566 F 119.

24. Pausanias: 10.4.10 (trans. W. H. S. Jones, LCL); for the practice of pouring liquids into the tomb, comparative material in the commentary of Sir James Frazer, *Pausanias's Description of Greece* 5 (London, 1898) 227–230.

25. Delphi: *Fouilles de Delphes* 3, 4, pt. 2, 218–220 (*Syll.*³ 361). Historical background: William W. Tarn, *Antigonos Gonatas* (Oxford, 1913) 95, 118. Site of the shrine: Jeremy McInerney, "The Phokikon and the Hero Archegetes," *Hesperia* 66 (1997) 193–207, placing it at Patronis northwest of Daulis. Heroes in the Roman period: below, ch. 6.

26. Burial in Sicyon: Plut. *Arat.* 53. *Hêrôon:* Paus. 2.8.1, 2.9.6. Son of Asclepius: 2.10.3.

27. "Last of the Greeks": Plut. *Philop.* 1.7. Burial: *Philop.* 31.3–9; Diod. Sic. 29.18; cf. Livy, 39.50.9, calling the honors *diuini,* presumably a translation of *isotheoi;* for this term as implying a level less than godhead, Nock, *Essays* 2.724–725. Inscription: *IG* 5.2, 432 (*Syll.*³ 624).

28. *SEG* 53 (2003) 40–42; cf. Christopher Jones, "Events surrounding the bequest of Pergamon to Rome and the revolt of Aristonicos," *Journal of Roman Archaeology* 17 (2004) 482–483.

29. Inscription: *IGR* 4.159, with the fundamental discussion of Jeanne and Louis Robert, *Bull. ép.* 1964, 227, pp. 180–181.

30. Equivalence of *oikistês* and *ktistês:* Louis Robert, *Hellenica* 4 (1948) 116; *Bull. ép.* 1974, 404. Mithridates: Hugo Hepding, "Mithridates von Pergamon," *Athenische Mitteilungen* 34 (1909) 329–340 (*IGR* 4.1682); Mikhail Rostovtzeff, *Social and Economic History of the Hellenistic World* (Oxford, 1957) 821–822, 1527–1528. For other "new heroes" of the same type, claiming not descent but similarity of achievement, Louis Robert, "Une épigramme satirique d'Automédon," *OMS* 6.446–447 (*REG*, 1981).

31. Zoilus: Robert, "Inscriptions d'Aphrodisias," *OMS* 6.413–432 (*Ant. Class.*, 1966). His monument: Robert R. R. Smith, *The Monument of C. Julius Zoilos* (Mainz am Rhein, 1999).

32. Eurycles: Glen W. Bowersock, "Eurycles of Sparta," *JRS* 51 (1961) 112–118; cf. *PIR*² I 301 (Eurycles), 302 (his descendant C. Iulius Eurycles Herculanus).

33. For later honors to valiant Greeks, note Mnesiboulos of Elateia about 170 (Paus. 10.34.5, *Syll.*³ 871); also the Athenian "greater than Leonides" of *IG* 2².13172, perhaps of the third century.

4. Athletes, Poets, Philosophers

1. Pl. *Meno* 81B = Pindar fr. 133 Race (above, ch. 1 at n. 16).

2. Oebatas: Paus. 6.3.8, 7.17.6–7, 7.17.13–14. For early hero-athletes, Joseph Fontenrose, "The Hero as Athlete," *California Studies in Classical Antiquity* 1 (1968) 73–104; François Bohringer, "Cultes d'Athlètes en Grèce classique," *Revue des Etudes Anciennes* 81 (1979) 5–18; Bruno Currie, "Euthymos of Locri," *JHS* 112 (2002) 24–44.

3. Euthymos: Callim. fragments 85–86 Pfeiffer with *diegesis* ad loc.; Oen. Gad. in Eus. *Praep. Evang.* 5.34.15–16 = Jürgen Hammerstaedt, *Die Orakelkritik des Kynikers Oenomaus* (Frankfurt, 1988) fr. 2.

4. Callim. fr. 98 with *diegesis*, fr. 99 = Pliny, *Nat. Hist.* 7.152; Paus. 6.6.4–6. Inscription: *Inschriften von Olympia* 144; in general, Currie, "Euthymos of Locri."

5. Paus. 6.11.2–9 (trans. W. H. S. Jones, LCL, adapted); other important texts are Dio Chrys. 31.95–97, Luc. *Deor. Conc.* 39.

6. Theagenes "god" in Hellenistic period: Paul Bernard and François Salviat, "Inscriptions de Thasos," *BCH* 86 (1962) 594 no. 14. In Roman period: *IG* 12 Suppl. (1939) 425; Christiane Dunant and Jean Pouilloux, *Recherches sur l'Histoire et les Cultes de Thasos* 2 (Paris, 1958) no. 322; Bernard and Salviat, "Inscriptions de Thasos," *BCH* 91 (1967) 579 no. 26.

7. Principal texts: Plut. *Rom.* 28.5–6; Paus. 6.9.6–8; Oen. Gad. fr. 2.2–14 Hammerstaedt; Or. C. *Celsum* 3.25; later sources in Fontenrose, "The Hero as Athlete" 74 n. 1.

8. *Anagyrasios daimôn:* Johannes Toepffer, "*Anagyrasios daimon,*" *RE* 1 (1894) 2027; Rudolf Kassel and Colin Austin, eds., *Poetae Comici Graeci* 3.2, frag. 41–66 (Aristophanes' *Anagyros*).

9. *Od.* 22.344–349 (trans. Augustus T. Murray and George C. Dimock, LCL). *Theios:* Ludwig Bieler, *Theios Aner: Das Bild des "göttlichen Menschen" in Spätantike und Frühchristentum* (Vienna, 1935) 9–13.

10. Ar. *Rhet.* 2.23.1, 1398b = Diskin Clay, *Archilochos Heros: The Cult of Poets in the Greek Polis* (Washington, D.C., 2004), 99 n. 1, with earlier bibliography.

11. Blind man: *H. Apoll.* 172. Gymnasium: *Corpus Inscriptionum Graecarum* 2221 = Georg Kaibel, *Epigrammata Graeca* 860. Sacrifice: *Certamen* 307. Julian: *Or.* 7, 210 a (Herbert W. Parke and Donald E. W. Wormell, *The Oracles of Apollo* [Oxford, 1956] 2.128 no. 320).

12. Homer in Smyrna: Cecil J. Cadoux, *Ancient Smyrna* (Oxford, 1938) 209–212. Cicero: *Arch.* 19 (Clay, *Archilochos* 137 T 1). Strabo: 14.1.37, 646 C (Clay, *Archilochos* 141 T 14). *Xoanon:* Robert, *OMS* 5.763 (*CRAI* 1981). Coins: Carlo Heyman, "Homer on Coins from Smyrna," *Studia Paulo Naster oblata* I (Leuven, 1982) 161–174; Dietrich O. A. Klose, *Die Münzprägung von Smyrna in der römischen Kaiserzeit* (Berlin, 1987) 34–36. Archilochos: see below.

13. Epigram: Lloyd-Jones and Parsons, *Suppl. Hell.* no. 979 (Clay, *Archilochos* 139 T 7). *Agalma:* Ael. *Var. Hist.* 13.22 (Clay, *Archilochos* 139 T 6). In general, P. M. Fraser, *Ptolemaic Alexandria* (Oxford, 1972) 1.611, 2.862–863.

14. Archelaus: Doris Pinkwart, *Das Relief des Archelaos von Priene* (Kallmünz, 1965); Paul Zanker, *The Mask of Socrates* (Berkeley, Los Angeles, London, 1995) 159–162; Clay, *Archilochos* 91–92. Cup from Pompeii: Ulrico Pannuti, *L'Apoteosi d'Omero, Monumenti Antichi* 3.2 (Rome, 1984).

15. Hesiod and the Muses: *Theog.* 1–115. *Hesiodeioi: IG* 7.1785 (*Syll.*[3] 1118; Clay, *Archilochos* 136 T 2); on the cult of Hesiod, Marie-Claude Beaulieu, "L'Héroïsation du Poète Hésiode," *Kernos* 17 (2004) 103–117. Miletos: *Inschriften von Didyma* 181, with the discussion of Jeanne and Louis Robert, *Bull. ép.* 1955, 196, p. 260. Platonists of Athens: Plut. *Quaest. conviv.* 8.1, 717 B; Porph. *Vita Plot.* 2. Statius: *Silv.* 4.4.54–55, with the commentary of Kathleen M. Coleman.

16. Coins: *BMC Troas* 200 nos. 165–70; *SNG Copenhagen,* Mytilene nos. 408, 409, 426; Clay, *Archilochos* 150–151. Inscription of Olympos: *TAM* 2.3, 1021.

17. Honors to Archilochos on Paros: Nikolaos M. Kontoleon, "Neai Epigraphai peri tou Archilochou ek Parou," *Archaiologikê Ephêmeris* 1952 (1955) 32–95 (*Bull. ép.* 1955, 178; 1962, 261; 1965, 302); W. Lambrinudakis and M. Wörrle, "Ein hellenistisches Reformgesetz aus Paros," *Chiron* 13 (1983) 293–94; Clay, *Archilochos* 9–39. The relief: Rhea N. Thönges-Stringaris, "Das griechische Totenmahl," *Ath. Mitt.* 80 (1965) 12, 73 no. 33 with pl. 3; Clay, *Archilochos* pl. 13. Demeas: *IG* 12.5, 445; *IG* 12 Suppl. (1939) 212–224 = *FGrHist* 502.

18. Andrew Connolly, "Was Sophocles Heroised as Dexion?" *JHS* 118 (1998) 1–21. Ister: Stefan Radt, ed., *Tragicorum Graecorum Fragmenta 4: Sophocles* (Göttingen, 1977) Testimonium 1, 17 = *FGrHist* 334 F 48. Byzantine lexica: Radt, Testimonium 69 (I have slightly altered Connolly's translation). Sophocles' public activity: Radt, Testimonium 18–27 ("Officia publica"). Brasidas: Aristotle, *Eth. Nic.* 5.7, 1124 B.

19. Pythagoras: *BMC Ionia,* Samos nos. 237, 286; *SNG* Copenhagen, *Ionia* no. 1733; *SNG* von Aulock no. 2317. Anaxagoras: *BMC Ionia* Clazomenae nos. 102, 125; *SNG* Copenhagen, *Ionia* no. 107. Bias: Diog. Laert. 1.82, *Inschriften von Priene* 111.245, 113.88, 117.34; Clay, *Archilochos* 131–132.

20. *Hêrôon:* Cass. Dio 77.18.4 (Christopher Jones, ed., *Philostratus: Apollonius of Tyana,* LCL 3, 89 no. 5). Philostratus' verdict: *Vit. Soph.* 1.21, p. 88 Wright. Oracle: *Theosoph. Tueb.* 44. Eunapius: *Vit. Philos.* 2.1.4 (Jones, *Philostratus: Apollonius of Tyana,* LCL 3, nos. 6, 15, 38).

21. Inscription: *IG* 12.7, 53 (*Syll.*[3] 889: Amorgos).

5. Private Heroes

1. Boutes: above, ch. 2 at n. 10. Kudrogenes: Ernst Pfuhl and Hans Möbius, *Die Ostgriechischen Grabreliefs* (Mainz am Rhein, 1977/1979) 2 no. 1520. For the development from heroic dedications to "Totenmahlreliefs," Rhea N. Thönges-Stringaris, "Das Griechische Totenmahl," *Ath. Mitt.* 80 (1965) 61–62.

2. Ulrich von Wilamowitz-Moellendorff, *Die Glaube der Hellenen* 2 (Berlin, 1932) 19, "Es ist später zu einer Erweiterung des Heroenglaubens gekommen, indem er nur noch bedeutet, dass dem Toten eine Fortdauer nach dem Tode gewährt sein soll, und die Hinterbliebenen schreiben es ihm auf den Grabstein. Hinz und Kunz wird nun erhöht. An ein Fortwirken denkt niemand. Es ist so formelhaft wie 'der selige P. P.'" Arthur D. Nock, "The Cult of Heroes," *Essays on Religion and the Ancient World* 2 (Cambridge, Mass., 1972) 842. For a very similar view to that taken here, that the word "hero" had true religious value and was not merely an empty compliment or a periphrasis for "the late," Fritz Graf, *Nordionische Kulte* (Schweizerisches Institut in Rom, 1985) 127–135; so also Dennis D. Hughes, "Hero Cult, Heroic Honors, Heroic Dead: Some Developments in the Hellenistic and Roman Periods," in Robin Hägg, ed., *Ancient Greek Hero Cult, Svenska Institutet i Athen, Series in 8°,* 16 (Stockholm, 1999) 167–175.

3. Louis Robert in Jean des Gagniers, *Laodicée du Lycos: Le Nymphée* (Québec and Paris, 1969) 265, 351–357.

4. Conon: Homer A. Thompson and Richard E. Wycherley, *The Athenian Agora* 14 (Princeton, N.J., 1972) 160.

5. *IG* 12.3, 330, especially B 7–25 (Epicteta's intentions), 61–106 (association, procession), 177–202 (offerings); Tullia Ritti, *Iscrizioni e Rilievi greci nel Museo Maffeiano* (Rome, 1981) no. 31; Andreas Wittenburg, *Il Testamento di Epikteta* (Trieste, 1990).

6. *IG* 12.7, 515; *IGR* 4.1000; Bernhard Laum, *Stiftungen in der griechischen und römischen Antike* (Berlin and Leipzig, 1914) 2.57–63 no. 50; Franciszek Sokolowski,

Lois sacrées des cités grecques: Supplément (Paris, 1962) 116–119 no. 61; Hughes, "Hero cult," 169. For monthly contests, cf. Dittenberger on *OGIS* 339, n. 19.

7. Frederik Poulsen, Konstantinos Rhomaios, *Erster vorläufiger Bericht über die dänisch-griechischen Ausgrabungen von Kalydon* (Copenhagen, 1927) 51–84; Ejnar Dyggve, Frederik Poulsen, Konstantinos Rhomaios, *Das Heroon von Kalydon* (Copenhagen, 1934). Inscription: *IG* 9.1.1² 141; Dyggve, Poulsen, and Rhomaios, 65–66. Sculptures: Poulsen and Rhomaios, 57–73; Dyggve, Poulsen, and Rhomaios, 73–89. On the evolution of *hêrôa* in the Hellenistic period, Ingrid Kader, "Heroa und Memorialbauten," in Michael Wörrle and Paul Zanker, eds., *Stadtbild und Bürgerbild im Hellenismus* (Munich, 1995) 199–229.

8. Shrine of Tullia: David R. Shackleton Bailey, "Tullia's Fane," *Cicero's Letters to Atticus* 5 (Cambridge, Eng., 1966), appendix III. For *apotheosis* as a form of heroization, Christopher Jones, "A Hellenistic Cult-Association," *Chiron* 38 (2008) 195–204.

9. Peter Herrmann and Kemal Z. Polatkan, *Das Testament des Epikrates und andere neue Inschriften aus dem Museum von Manisa* (Vienna, 1969) 7–36, lines 33–35, 49–51, 93–105; *Bull. ép.* 1970, 512. For offerings of roses to the dead, Christina Kokkinia, "Rosen für die Toten im griechischen Raum," *Mus. Helv.* 56 (1999) 204–221.

10. Snake: Pfuhl-Möbius, 2 no. 1578 (Pergamon, 2nd century B.C.E.).

11. Herodes' mourning: Lucian, *Demonax* 24. Relief from Brauron: Georges Daux, "Chronique des Fouilles," *BCH* 87 (1963) 710 fig. 10. Contests: *IG* 2/3² 3968. For this argument, Louis Robert, "Deux inscriptions de l'Époque imperiale en Attique II: Un Concours et Hérode Atticus," *OMS* 5.130–135 (*American Journal of Philology* 1979).

12. Thus Charles Michel, art. "Coena" in Charles Daremberg, Edmond Saglio, *Dictionnaire des Antiquités grecques et romaines* 1 (Paris, 1877) 1273, "les femmes et les enfants, lorsque par hasard ils prenaient part à un dîner où des hommes se trouvaient réunis, ce qui n'était pas l'usage des Grecs, mangeaient toujours assis," citing Xen. *Sympos.* 1.8, Euangelos fr. 1 (Kassel-Austin, *Poetae Comici Graeci* 5.184), Dio Chrys. 7.65, 67, Lucian, *Sympos.* 8. On the change of custom at Rome, Shackleton Bailey on Cicero, *ad Fam.* 9.26.2 (*Cicero: Epistulae ad familiares* 2.354), citing Val. Max. 2.1.2. In Petronius' *Cena Trimalchionis*, the women recline.

13. E. Gàbrici, "Stele sepolcrali di Lilibeo a Forma di Heroon," *Monumenti Antichi* 33 (1929) 42–59, with pl. II 1; art. "Lilibeo" by I. Marconi-Bovio, *Enciclopedia dell' Arte Antica* 4 (1961) 626–630, especially plate facing 626.

14. Plut. *Agis-Cleom.* 39. For Plutarch's distrust of instant heroization, below, ch. 6 at n. 2.

15. Theophrastus: Theophr. *Char.* 16.1, with the commentary of James Diggle, *Theophrastus:* Characters (Cambridge, Eng., 2004) 355–357. Apollonius: Wolfgang Blümel, *Inschriften der Rhodischen Peraea* no. 209, 7–10 (Peek, *Griechische Vers-Inschriften* 1260).

16. Hans F. Gadow, "Snakes," *Encyclopaedia Britannica*[11] 25 (Cambridge, Eng., 1911) 289, right-hand column.

17. Horse: Ludwig Malten, "Das Pferd im Totenglauben," *Jahrbuch des Instituts* 29 (1914) 179–256 (learned but fanciful); Alexandrina Cermanovi-Kusmanovic et al., "Heros equitans," *LIMC* 6.1, 1019–1081. Kudrogenes: above n. 1. Riders: Pfuhl-Möbius 2 pp. 310–348. Women riders: Pfuhl-Möbius 2 nos. 1419–1421.

18. Antinoos: Hugo Meyer, *Antinoos: Die archäologischen Denkmäler* (Munich, 1991) pl. 115, nos. 18, 19, 21–23. Thracian rider at Odessos: Georgius Mihailov, *Inscriptiones Graecae in Bulgaria repertae* 1² 78 ter, with pl. 51, and in general Ivana Popovic, art. "Heros Equitans," *LIMC* 6.1, 1073–1081. *Sôzôn*: Marielouise Cremer, art. "Sozon," *LIMC* 8.1, 1148–1149. Kakasbos: Robert, "Un Dieu anatolien: Kakasbos," *Hellenica* 3 (Paris, 1946) 38–76; Pascale Linant de Bellefonds, art. "Kakasbos," *LIMC* 6.1, 1082–1084.

19. Sopater: Pfuhl-Möbius 1 no. 116, cf. nos. 235, 266, al. Lais: Pfuhl-Möbius 2 no. 1581. "Kindly hero": Pfuhl-Möbius 2 no. 1363, rider; cf. 1 no. 200, standing figure; 2 no. 1378, rider and standing figure; 2 no. 2224, two opposing dolphins. "New hero": Pfuhl-Möbius 2 no. 1322, rider. "Manifest hero": Pfuhl-Möbius 2 no. 1349: rider, altar, snake, cf. no. 1389, two riders approaching an altar before which stands a woman making a gesture of adoration. Legionary: Pfuhl-Möbius 1 no. 306.

20. Dionysios: Pfuhl-Möbius 1 no. 640 (Peek, *Griechische Vers-Inschriften* no. 768); for the *hêrôon* of Calydon, below. Ephesus: Pfuhl-Möbius 1 no. 869 (Peek no. 677). Samos: Pfuhl-Möbius 2 no. 1821 (Peek no. 1154). Miletoupolis: Pfuhl-Möbius 2 no. 1617, pl. 235 (Peek no. 718).

21. *IG* 12.7, 447; Michel Sève, "Un Enterrement public dans une Épigramme d'Aigialè d'Amorgos," *REG* 109 (1996) 683–688.

22. Stratonice: Pfuhl-Möbius I no. 808; R. Merkelbach, J. Stauber, *Steinepigramme aus dem griechischen Osten* 1 (Stuttgart and Leipzig, 1998) 348, no. 03/02/67 (Ephesos). Julia: Pfuhl-Möbius 2 no. 2088 with pl. 301 (Peek 438a).

23. Poem of Marcellus: *Inscriptiones Graecae Urbis Romae* 3.1155, 8–9, 41–45; Wilamowitz, "Marcellus von Side," *Kleine Schriften* 2 (Berlin, 1971) 192–228 (*Sitzungsber. Akad. Berlin*, 1928).

24. Ael. Ar. 31.15, 18 (pp. 215–216 Keil); "Menander": 414, 16, 421, 16 Spengel = 162, 176 Russell-Wilson.

25. Tombs erected for own use: e.g., *MAMA* 6.209, 213 (Apamea Cibotos). On the various names for "tomb," Jadwiga Kubinska, *Les Monuments funéraires dans les inscriptions grecques d'Asie Mineure* (Warsaw, 1968), especially 28–31 on *hêrôon*.

26. Adolf Wilhelm, "Ein attisches Vereingesetz," *Abhandlungen und Beiträge zur griechischen Inschriftenkunde* 2 (Leipzig, 1985) 1–5 (*Serta Harteliana* [Vienna, 1896]); *IG* 2/3² 1369; Louis Robert, "Deux Inscriptions," *OMS* 5.123–129. For sim-

ilar arrangements elsewhere, Wilhelm cites *IG* 7.2725 (Acraephiae, Boeotia), and Eugen Petersen, Felix von Luschan, *Reisen in Lykien, Milyas und Kibyratis* 2 (Vienna, 1889) 36 (Myra, Lycia).

27. Peplos: Christopher Jones, "A Deed of Foundation from the Territory of Ephesos," *JRS* 73 (1983) 116–26 (*SEG* 33, 946). Pisidia: Rudolf Heberdey and Wilhelm Wilberg, "Grabbauten von Termessos in Pisidien," *Jahresh. Öest. Arch. Inst.* 3 (1900) 205–207; Heberdey, *TAM* 3.713; Kubinska, *Monuments funéraires* 26–28. Calocairos: *TAM* 2.2, 466.

28. *MAMA* 6.224 (Trophimos), 237 (intoners of psalms).

29. See below, ch. 7.

6. Greek Heroes in a Roman World

1. *Thes.* 1.

2. *Rom.* 28.8–10. On Plutarch and deification, Christopher Jones, *Plutarch and Rome* (Oxford, 1971) 123–124; Glen W. Bowersock, "Greek Intellectuals and the Imperial Cult," in Willem den Boer, ed., *Le Culte des souverains dans l'Empire romain, Entretiens Hardt* 19 (Geneva, 1973) 187–191.

3. Plutarch's son Chairon: *Consol. ad uxor.* 609 D. Hero Chairon: Paus. 9.40.5. For "herophoric names," Louis Robert, *Noms Indigènes dans l'Asie-Mineure Gréco-Romaine* (Paris, 1963) 622 s.v. "héros et anthroponymes"; Robert Parker, "Theophoric Names and the History of Greek Religion," *Proceedings of the British Academy* 104 (2000) 56. Address to Timon: *de sera num. vind.* 558 A-B (trans. Phillip De Lacy and Benedict Einarson, LCL, slightly altered). Biographies of Heracles, Daiphantus, Aristomenes, Epaminondas: *Lamprias Catalog* nos. 34 (Heracles), 38 (Daiphantus), 39 (Aristomenes), 7 (Epaminondas). On the cult of Aristomenes and Epaminondas in imperial Messene, Petros Themelis, *Hêrôes kai Hêrôa stê Messênê* (Athens, 2000) 28–58.

4. Themistocles: Plut. *Them.* 32.6. Aratus: above, ch. 3 at n. 26.

5. Ajax: Philostr. *Her.* 8.1. Alcibiades: Athenaeus 13.574 F; on the location of Melissa, Louis Robert, *A travers l'Asie Mineure* (Paris, 1980) 258–291. Panhellenion: on the heroic claims of the members, Christopher Jones, "A Letter of Hadrian to Naryka (Eastern Locris)," *JRA* 19 (2006) 154–155.

6. Lamprias: *IG* 4^2.82–86, cf. *SEG* 35 (1985) 304–05; on the chronology, Antony S. Spawforth, "Families at Roman Sparta and Epidaurus," *Ann. Brit. Sch. Athens* 80 (1985) 249–258. Lysander: Christian Habicht, *Gottmenschentum und griechische Städte*^{2} (Göttingen, 1970) 3–7, 243–244; *IG* 12.6, 334. Consolation decrees: Louis Robert, *Hellenica* 3 (Paris, 1946) 10–28 (the "hero" Statilius Apollinaris); Robert, *Hellenica* 13 (Paris, 1965) Index s.v. "Consolation (décrets de)."

7. Christian Habicht, *Altertümer von Pergamon* VIII 3: *Die Inschriften des Asklepieions* (Berlin, 1969) no. 134 with pl. 41.

8. Denis Feissel and Gilbert Dagron, *Inscriptions de Cilicie* (Paris, 1987) 72 with pl. 30; cf. the sanctuary and cult-statue dedicated by Prusa to the mother of Dio Chrysostom, Dio Prus. 44.3. For the centering of "hero," note also Hugo Hepding, "Die Arbeiten zu Pergamon 1904–1905: Die Inschriften," *Ath. Mitt.* 32 (1907) 331–334 no. 64.

9. Habicht, *Inschriften des Asklepieions* no. 2.

10. Byzas: Carmen Arnold-Biucchi, *LIMC* 3 (1986) 174. Marcus: Philostr. *Vit. Soph.* 1.24, 527–531 Ol.; *PIR*² M 465; Louis Robert in Nezih Firatlı, *Les Stèles funéraires de Byzance* (1964) 137; Poseidon's hair: H. Bulle, "Poseidon in der Kunst," in W. H. Roscher, *Ausführliches Lexikon der griechischen und römischen Mythologie* 3.2 (Leipzig, 1897–1909) 2860, "In later art the god has the same huge mass of curls and the same full flowing beard as his brother Zeus, except that his hair is matted so as to be more wild and unruly" (my translation).

11. Coins of Marcus: Edith Schönert-Geiss, *Die Münzprägung von Byzantion II*: *Kaiserzeit* (Berlin and Amsterdam, 1972) 170, Index 2, "Beamtennamen" s.v. "Memmius Marcus" and "Memmius Marcus Heros." "Heroes" and "heroines" holding posthumous office: Louis Robert, "Recherches épigraphiques," *OMS* 2.810–812 (*Revue des Études Anciennes* 1960), *Documents de l'Asie mineure méridionale* (Paris, 1966) 83–85. Aphrodisias: Christopher Jones, "Two inscribed Monuments of Aphrodisias," *Arch. Anz.* 1994, 2, 470–471; below, appendix.

12. Inscription: Elena Miranda, *Iscrizioni greche d'Italia: Napoli* 1 (Rome, 1990) no. 44. "Father," etc.: Christopher Jones, "*Trophimos* in an Inscription of Erythrai," *Glotta* 67 (1989) 194–197.

13. Glen W. Bowersock, *Fiction as History* (Berkeley, Los Angeles, London, 1994) index s.v. "Homeric revisionism."

14. Homer: *Iliad* 2.695–710. Philostratus: *Her.* 9.1 (hill), 9.6 (statue); Christopher Jones, "Philostratus' *Heroikos* and its Setting in Reality," *JHS* 121 (2001) 141–149.

15. Sergej B. Ochotnikov, "Achilleus auf der Insel Leuke," in Joachim Hupe, ed., *Der Achilleus-Kult im nördlichen Schwarzmeerraum* (Rahden/Westf., 2006), 49–87.

16. Hld. 2.34–35 (Theagenes' appearance), 10.30 (bullfight). Thessalian bull-wrestling *(taurokathapsia)*: Louis Robert, *OMS* 7.515–525 (*Journal des Savants* 1982).

7. Antinoos

1. The literature is enormous. Among older treatments, Lorentz Dietrichson, *Antinoos: Eine kunstarchäologische Untersuchung* (Christiania, 1884) 333–346 is an

invaluable collection of literary texts; for the coins, Gustave Blum, "Numismatique d'Antinoos," *Journ. internat. d'Archéol. numism.* 16 (1914) 33–70. Recent discussions include Royston Lambert, *Beloved and God: The Story of Hadrian and Antinous* (London, 1984); Hugo Meyer, *Antinoos: Die archäologischen Denkmäler* (Munich, 1991); Caroline Vout, *Power and Eroticism in Imperial Rome* (Cambridge, Eng. and New York, 2007) 52–135.

2. First meeting: Anthony R. Birley, *Hadrian: The Restless Emperor* (London and New York, 1997) 158, dates this tentatively to "the autumn of 123 or spring of 124," rejecting a possible meeting in 117, since "Antinous was surely too young then—and Hadrian too preoccupied—for any significant encounter." On Antinooupolis, see below.

3. Text of the obelisk: Hugo Meyer, ed., *Der Obelisk des Antinoos* (Munich, 1994). For "Osiris-Antinoos," Meyer, *Obelisk* 41, 53, 65; burial place, 61; cult in Antinooupolis, 53; flower: Athen. 15, 677 D. Dio: 69.11.4. For poems preserved on papyrus attributing some of the same characteristics to Antinoos, *POxy.* 50.3537; 63.4352; for a papyrus referring to his *ektheôsis*, *POxy.* 31.2553.

4. Foundation and tribes of Antinooupolis: Michael Zahrnt, "Antinoopolis in Ägypten: Die hadrianische Gründung und ihre Privilegien in der neueren Forschung," *ANRW* 2.10.1 (Berlin and New York, 1988) 669–706; Meyer, *Obelisk* 159. Hegesippos: Eus. *Hist. Eccl.* 4.8.2. Clement: Clem. *Protrept.* 4.49.1. Justin: *Apol.* 29.4 = Eus. *Hist. Eccl.* 4.8.3. Origen: *Contra Cels.* 3.36. Love-spell: *SEG* 26 (1976) 1717.

5. Paus. 8.9.7–8 (my translation): I have translated *enomisthê* as a perfect (Smyth, section 1940, "Aorist for Perfect"), and *espoudasthê* as "favored" to maintain the ambiguity of the word: LSJ cite Plutarch *Them.* 5.3 (a musician favored by the Athenians), *Cimon* 4.9 (two women "courted" by Cimon *erôtikôs*). "Stones" refers, as often, to plaques of colored marble used as revetment. Essential discussion of this passage: Louis Robert, *A travers l'Asie Mineure* (Paris, 1980) 132–138.

6. Herculanus: *IG* 5.2, 281 (*Syll.*³ 841). Statue: *IG* 5.2, 312, where *êrato* must be the aorist middle of *aeirô*, "raise," not *eramai*, "love." On both these texts, Robert, *A travers* 135–136, correctly understanding *êrato* as "enlevé."

7. Mysteries: *IGR* 3.73 = *I. Klaudiu Polis* 65; on the consular, M. Domitius Euphemus, *PIR*² D 146. Altar: *I. Klaudiu Polis* 56. Contests: Robert, *A travers* 132–133. Tribes: Christian Marek, *Mus. Helv.* 59 (2002) 31–50 (*SEG* 52 [2002] 1231).

8. Coinage: Blum, "Numismatique d'Antinoos"; several of the coins also in Lambert, *Beloved*, pl. 46–48. Sites in Asia: Aeolis: Cyme, Mytilene. Bithynia: Bithynion-Claudiopolis, Nicomedia, Tieion, Chalcedon. Mysia: Cyzicus, Adramyttion, Hadrianoutherae, Hadrianopolis-Stratonicaea. Lydia: Philadelphia, Sardis, Tmolus, Sala (not securely placed, but between Lydia and Phrygia).

9. Antinoea: Jeanne and Louis Robert, *Bull. ép.* 1952, pp. 192–193. Athens: *IG* 2/3.2042, 9; 2046, 14; 2049, 22, 24, etc. Argos: *IG* 4.590, 11. Tomis: *IGR* 1.634. Statue

at Delphi: Gustave Blum, "L'Antinoos de Delphes," *BCH* 37 (1913) 323–339; Meyer, *Antinoos* 36–38 no. I 15.

10. Aristotimos: Bernadette Puech, "Prosopographie des Amis de Plutarque," *ANRW* 2.33.6 (Berlin and New York, 1992) 4837–4839. (M. Antonius) Polemo: Philostr. *Vit. Soph.* 1.25, 530–535 Olearius; *PIR*[2] A 862. Julius Saturninus: *IGR* 3.171; Werner Eck, *Senatoren von Vespasian bis Hadrian* (Munich, 1970) 224.

11. On appellations such as "new Dionysos," Arthur D. Nock, *Essays on Religion and the Ancient World* 2 (Cambridge, Mass., 1972) 148–149. Imperial mysteries: Louis Robert, "Recherches épigraphiques," *OMS* 2.837–838 (*Revue des Etudes Anciennes* 1960); Simon Price, *Rituals and Power* (Cambridge, Eng., 1984) 190–191.

12. Isochrysos: *IG* 5.2, 312 (above, n. 6). Lanuvium: *Corpus Inscriptionum Latinarum* 14.2112 = Hermann Dessau, *Inscriptiones Latinae Selectae* 7212. Relief: Meyer, *Antinoos* 96–98, no. 175.

13. Re-Harakte and blessing of Hadrian: Meyer, *Obelisk* 31; Hadrian and Sabina, 35, 37. Coin of Hadrianoutherae: Hans von Fritze, *Münzen Mysiens* (1913) 569–570 with pl. 9, 25; Louis Robert, *Documents d'Asie Mineure* (Paris, 1987) 440.

14. On Alexander and Glycon: Lucian, *Alexander the False Prophet* (LCL 3.173–253); Louis Robert, *A travers* 393–421; Christopher Jones, *Culture and Society in Lucian* (Cambridge, Mass., 1986) ch. 14; Ulrich Victor, ed., *Lukian von Samosata: Alexandros oder der Lügenprophet* (Leiden, New York, Köln, 1997).

8. Heroes and Saints

1. Aug. *Civ. Dei* 10. 21. In this chapter I use "pagan" for those who were neither Christians nor Jews, whether or not they consciously resisted Christianity.

2. On the question of a link between saints and heroes, Wolfgang Speyer, art. "Heros," *Reallex. für Ant. und Christ.* 14 (1988) 873–875 (bibliography). For similarities between the pagan and Christian veneration of the dead, Martin P. Nilsson, *Geschichte der griechischen Religion*[3] (Munich, 1974) 544, 547.

3. Tychon: H. Usener, *Der Heiliger Tychon* (Leipzig, 1907). Nestor: Hugo Mühlestein, "Jung Nestor, Jung David," *Antike und Abendland* 17 (1974) 173–190. Delehaye: *Les Origines du Culte des Martyrs* (Brussels, 1933) 404–417, especially 414. So also Peter Brown, *The Cult of the Saints: Its Rise and Function in Latin Christianity* (Chicago, 1981) 5–6, "In Christian belief, the grave, the memory of the dead, and the religious ceremonial that might surround this memory were placed within a totally different structure of relations between God, the dead, and the living."

4. First Commandment: *Exod.* 20.3–4. Golden Calf: *Exod.* 32. Psalms: 95.5, 115.4, 8. Paul: *I Cor.* 8.4, *Rom.* 1.25.

5. Socrates: Justin, *I Apol.* 5.3 (ed. Charles Munier, *SC* 507, 138). "Son of Zeus": I *Apol.* 21 (SC 507, 186–190). Demons behind Greek myths: *I Apol.* 54 (*SC* 507, 270–272).

6. Tatian, *Apol.* 21.1, 32.2–3, with the translation of Molly Whittaker (Oxford, 1982), slightly altered.

7. Ps.-Justin, ed. Christoph Riedweg, *Ps.-Justin (Markell von Ankyra?), Ad Graecos de vera religione* (Basel, 1994), *Coh.* 2.4 (gods), 28.2 (Egypt), 17.2 (*Il.* 2.204 and monotheism), 28.3 (Creation), 28.4 (Alcinoos and Paradise). Cf. Riedweg, 51–53 (date of Ps. Justin), 101–108 (his attitude to Homer).

8. Prud. *Cath.* 6.113–114. *Polyesthlos: SEG* 1 (1923) 453. *Agakleitos: IG* 14.2379. Anastasius: *SEG* 36 (1986) 1344. Constantius: Johannes B. De Rossi, *Inscriptiones Christianae urbis Romae* 1 (Rome, 1861) 265; Ernestus Diehl, *Inscr. Chr. Lat. Vet.* 1 (1961) no. 66; on the person, *PLRE* 2.319–320, Constantius 9.

9. Julian, *Ep.* 79 Bidez-Cumont = 19 Wright (LCL Julian 3.49; Wright's translation slightly altered).

10. Zos. 4.18.1–4. On Nestorius, *PLRE* 1.626, "Nestorius 2": on Syrianus, *PLRE* 2.1051, "Syrianus 2."

11. Megara: Adolf Wilhelm, "Simonideische Gedichte," *Abhandlungen zur griechischen Inschriftenkunde* (Leipzig, 1984) 30–38 (superseding the text in *IG* 7.53), whence Denys L. Page, *Further Greek Epigrams* (Cambridge, Eng., 1981) "Simonides" xvi (LCL Greek Lyric 3.532). On this inscription see also Gunnel Ekroth, *The Sacrificial Rituals of Greek Hero-Cults* (Liège, 2002) 77–78.

12. Glanville Downey, *A History of Antioch in Syria* (Princeton, N.J., 1961) 387–388.

13. [Plutarch,] *On the Education of Children* and *How the Young Should Study Poetry, mor.* 1 A–37 B (Frank C. Babbitt, ed., *Plutarch's Moralia*, LCL 1.1–197). Basil: Nigel G. Wilson, ed., *St. Basil on the Value of Greek Literature* (London, 1975).

14. Christian Habicht, "Spätantikes Grabepigramm aus Demetrias," in *Demetrias* 1 (1976) 199–203 (*SEG* 26 [1975–1976] 645).

15. Annaliese Kossatz-Deissmann, art. "Achilleus" *LIMC* 1 (1981) 56 (the myth), 65 no. 172 (central scene); Victorine von Gonzenbach, "Achillesplatte," in Herbert A. Cahn and Annemarie Kaufmann-Heinimann, eds., *Der spätrömische Silberschatz von Kaiseraugst* (Derendingen, 1984) 1.225–307. Sevso Treasure: Marlia M. Mango and Anna Bennett, *The Sevso Treasure, Part One, JRA* Supplementary Series 12,1 (Ann Arbor, Mich., 1994) 153–180. For this interpretation, Alan Cameron, "Young Achilles in the Roman World"; I am very grateful to the author for showing me this study in advance of publication.

Appendix

1. Rohde: *Psyche*[7, 8] (Tübingen, 1921) 257, "Zuletzt aber wurde es eine fast gedankenlos geübte Gewöhnung, selbst Privatpersonen bei Lebzeiten mit dem Heroentitel auszuzeichnen, heroische Ehren, wohl gar die Stiftung jährlich zu widerholender Wettspiele, Lebenden zu widmen" (my translation). "Debased habit": Simon Hornblower, *Mausolus* (Oxford and New York, 1982) 254. Cf. P. M. Fraser, *Rhodian Funerary Monuments* (Oxford, 1977) 78, "It indicates a further reduction of status that ἥρως was used as a hyperbolical form of praise to a living benefactor, from the fourth century onwards."

2. Reinach, "Temple d'Hadrien à Cyzique," *BCH* 14 (1890) 537, "L'hipparque éponyme porte le titre de ἥρως qui, dans l'épigraphie de Cyzique, est fréquemment donné à des hommes ou à des femmes, même de leur vivant."

3. Wilhelm: Rudolf Heberdey and Adolf Wilhelm, *Reisen in Kilikien* (Vienna, 1896) 153–154; see also Louis Robert, *Documents de l'Asie Mineure Méridionale* (Geneva and Paris, 1966) 83–85, citing the inscription now *Inschriften von Kyme* 102.

4. Aphrodisias: *SEG* 50 (2000) 1096, with the comments of Angelos Chaniotis on line 27.

5. Nero: Tac. *Ann.* 15.74.3. Hagnon: ch. 3 at n. 10. Euthymos of Locri: ch. 4 at n. 4.

6. Diod. Sic. 16.20.6. Diocles: Diod. Sic. 13.35.2. Honors conferred before death: Jeanne and Louis Robert, *Bull. ép.* 1966, 272, p. 400; *Bull. ép.* 1968, 444, p. 504 (Aeolian Cyme, showing that the city had a special burial-place reserved for benefactors). Diodorus Pasparos: Hugo Hepding, "Die Arbeiten zu Pergamon 1904–1905: Die Inschriften," *Ath. Mitt.* 32 (1907) 246–247, no. 4, 37–52 (*IGR* 4.292).

7. Demochares: Athen. 6.253A = *FGrHist* 75 F 1. Adeimantos: Louis Robert, "Adeimantos et la Ligue de Corinthe," *Hellenica* 2 (Paris, 1946) 15–33; Christian Habicht, *Gottmenschentum und griechische Städte*[2] (Munich, 1970) 55–56. Paeans for Demetrios and Antigonos: Philochoros, Athen. 15.697 A = *FGrHist* 328 F 165. Hermocles: Athen. 6.253 D-F = *FGrHist* 76 F 13 (Douris) = Johannes U. Powell, *Collectanea Alexandrina* (Oxford, 1925) 173–174. On the historical circumstances, Christian Habicht, *Athens from Alexander to Antony* (Cambridge, Mass., 1997) 79–80, 92–93.

8. Nicias: Bruno Keil, "Kyzikenisches," *Hermes* 32 (1897) 500 n. 1; *PIR*[2] N 84; Kostas Buraselis, *Kos: Between Hellenism and Rome* (Philadelphia, 2000) 55–60, with a list of the relevant inscriptions, 154–155. Xenophon: Buraselis, *Kos* 109–110. Compare the sacrifices at Aeolian Cyme marking the recovery *(sôtêria)* of the benefactress Archippe from a dangerous illness, *SEG* 33 (1983) 1038, 18.

9. Diodorus: 2.46.5, 45.5; 4.28.4, 50.2, etc. Cicero: *Ep. ad Att.* 1.17.9. Eusebius: *Contra Hieroclem* 28.1. Julian: *Hymn to the Sun* 26 (146B).

Index

Achaea, 33–34, 38–39, 68; in Homer, 3–4, 6

Achilles: in archaic poetry, 2–10, 13–14, 23, 26; as athletic model, 40; cult of, 14–15, 87–90; in Late Antiquity, 87–92; post-Homeric accounts of, 72–74, 91–92

Achilles Plate, 92

Adeimantos, Macedonian, 95

Aelius Aristides, 62–63

Aeneas, 4, 84–85

Aeolis, 79, 93–94

Agamemnon, 4, 14

Agônes. *See* Contests

Ajax "the Greater," 19, 68, 87

Ajax "the Lesser," 9

Alcibiades, 68

Alcidamas, 42, 44–45

Alcinoos, 4, 38, 87

Alcmena, 5

Alexander of Abonuteichos, 82–83

Alexander III of Macedon, 29, 31, 43, 76

Alexandria, 43, 56, 76

Alexandrian War, 35–36

Aleximachos of Aegiale, 51–52, 61

Amorgos, 51, 53, 68–69, 85

Amphipolis, veneration of Brasidas at, 1, 24–26, 30, 37, 45, 52; veneration of Hagnon at, 26, 94

Anagyrasios daimôn, 41

Anastasius I, emperor, 87–88

Anaxagoras, 46

Ancyra, cult of Antinoos at, 83

Androcrates of Plataea, 13, 21, 84

Antenoridai, 11

Antigonos I Monophthalmos, 28–29, 95

Antigonos II Gonatas, 32

Antinoos: association with other gods, 75–76, 80–81; on coins, 59, 79–80; cult in Bithynion and Mantinea, 78–79; cult in Egypt, 76, 78; cult in Italy, 76; obelisk of Antinoos, 76–77, 82; relationship to Hadrian, 75, 81–82

Antinooupolis, 75–79

Antonius Polemo, Marcus, 80

Aphrodisias, 36, 94

Aphrodite, 36, 53, 87, 95

Apollo, 9, 10, 11, 35, 44–45, 59, 62; oracle at Delphi, 19, 33, 39–40, 45; other oracles, 46, 69, 90

Apollonios, warrior-hero, 58

Apollonios of Metropolis, 34–35

Apollonius of Tyana, 46–47, 96

Apotheosis of Homer, 43

Aratus of Sicyon, 33–34, 68

Arcadia, 30, 34, 78–79

Arcesilas IV of Cyrene, 10–11

Arcesine, 85

Archelaos of Priene, 43

Archilochos of Paros, 42, 44–45, 50

Ares, 58, 87

Argonauts, 11, 13

Argos, 5, 9, 42, 69, 79

Aristogiton and Harmodius, 23, 29

Aristomenes, hero, 68

Aristonicos of Pergamon, 34–35

Aristoteles of Thera. *See* Battos

Aristotle, 25

REVEALING ANTIQUITY
G. W. Bowersock, General Editor